Intellectual Property Law in India

Intellectual Property Law in India

Fourth Edition

Tamali Sen Gupta

This book was originally published as a monograph in the International Encyclopaedia of Laws/Intellectual Property Law.

Founding Editor: Roger Blanpain
General Editor: Frank Hendrickx
Volume Editor: Hendrik Vanhees

Wolters Kluwer

Published by:
Kluwer Law International B.V.
PO Box 316
2400 AH Alphen aan den Rijn
The Netherlands
E-mail: lrs-sales@wolterskluwer.com
Website: www.wolterskluwer.com/en/solutions/kluwerlawinternational

Sold and distributed by:
Wolters Kluwer Legal & Regulatory U.S.
920 Links Avenue
Landisville, PA 17538
United States of America
E-mail: customer.service@wolterskluwer.com

ISBN 978-94-035-4638-4

e-Book: ISBN 978-94-035-4648-3
web-PDF: ISBN 978-94-035-4658-2

The Author

Dr Tamali Sen Gupta specializes in corporate law and laws relating to intellectual property. Dr Sen Gupta holds the following degrees: Doctor of Science of Law – JSD and Master of Science of Law – JSM, both from Stanford University, California. These are in addition to her BA (Economics) and LLB from the University of Delhi. She was admitted to the Bar in 1986 and has practised before the Supreme Court of India. Her core areas of practice have been intellectual property law, joint ventures, infrastructure contracts, media laws and other aspects of commercial law. Dr Sen Gupta is Managing Partner of T. Sen Gupta & Associates, a corporate law firm, providing corporate advisory services for inbound business in India. Dr Sen Gupta is involved with several initiatives on Intellectual Property Rights (IPRs), Trade-Related Aspects of Intellectual Property (TRIPS) and with the World Trade Organization (WTO) at New Delhi. She has been invited as a guest speaker at Stanford University, Berkeley University, Indian Law Institute, Indian Institute of International Law, International Management Institute, etc. She has published several articles on IPRs. Some publications are 'COVID Pandemic and Intellectual Property Rights', 2021; 'Protection of Intellectual Property in India and South Korea', 1991; 'Project Finance and Infrastructure', 2000; and 'Telecommunications Laws in India', 2005.

The Author

Table of Contents

Table of Contents

List of Abbreviations

CCA	Commercial Courts Act
CRI	Computer-Related Invention
IPAB	Intellectual Property Appellate Board
IPC	International Patent Classification
IPD	Intellectual Property Division
IPR	Intellectual Property Right
NBA	National Biodiversity Authority
NGO	Non-governmental Organization
PCT	Patent Cooperation Treaty
PPVFRA	Protection of Plant Varieties and Farmers Rights Authority
SMI & SSMI	Social Media Intermediaries and Significant Social Media Intermediaries
TRIPS	Trade-Related Aspects of Intellectual Property Rights
UK	United Kingdom
US	United States
USD	US Dollar
WCT	WIPO Copyright Treaty
WHO	World Health Organization
WIPO	World Intellectual Property Organization
WPPT	WIPO Performances and Phonograms Treaty
WTO	World Trade Organization

List of Abbreviations

General Introduction

Chapter 1. General Background

§1. Geography

1. India is the seventh-largest country in the world, with an area of 3,287,263 sq. km. The mainland comprises four geographic regions: namely, the Himalayan Range of mountains to the north, the Indo-Gangetic plains of the rivers Ganges and Indus, the Thar Desert region in the west and the southern peninsula. There is tremendous diversity in flora and fauna due to the country's location in different climatic zones, viz., high snow-covered mountains on its north, the alluvial Gangetic plains and the Deccan plateau spread over tropical and sub-tropical zones. India has a land frontier of about 15,200 km with a coastline of 7,516.6 km. The climate may be broadly included under tropical monsoon-type weather, although large areas also have a desert climate.

§2. Cultural Composition

2. The majority of the people are Hindus, followed by Muslims and Christians, who comprise the larger minority groups. The secular character of the country has made it a safe abode for many groups who escaped to India following persecution elsewhere in the world, including Parsis, Jews, Armenians, Chinese and, more recently, Tibetans escaping the Chinese invasion of Tibet. There is no uniform civil code, and each religious group is governed by their personal laws in relation to marriage, divorce, succession, inheritance, etc. Although Indians are racially and culturally extremely diverse, there is a common urban Indian culture that arose initially out of the widespread use of the English language and recently through the popular entertainment and music industries.

§3. Political System

3. India is a sovereign socialist secular democratic republic with a parliamentary system of government. The Constitution of India came into force on 26 January 1950 and provides for a parliamentary form of government. The President of India is the constitutional head of the executive. The country is governed by the Prime Minister, aided by the Council of Ministers, and the executive powers are vested in the Central Cabinet, headed by the Prime Minister. India has twenty-eight States and eight Union Territories. Each state is headed by a Governor and administered by a Council of State Ministers headed by the Chief Minister of the State. Elections based on adult franchise are held at two levels: for the Central Parliament and for each State Legislative Assembly. Apart from the twenty-eight States, India has eight Union Territories, some which are governed directly by the Central Government, while three have elected legislatures. Elections for the Jammu and Kashmir (one of the newly formed Union Territories) Legislative Assembly were held in 2024 along with the general election, following the delimitation of parliamentary and assembly constituencies of the newly formed Union Territory. Citizenship is by birth and can be extended to any person whose parents were born in the territory of India. The Citizenship Act, 1955, provides conditions for citizenship. Citizenship can also be acquired through naturalization, provision for which is made in the Citizenship Act. It was amended in 2019, to provide an accelerated pathway to Indian citizenship for persecuted religious minorities from Afghanistan, Bangladesh and Pakistan.

§4. Judicial System

4. India has a strong and effective rule of law with fundamental rights guaranteed by the Constitution of India. The Supreme Court of India and the High Courts have been vigilant in reinforcing the Rule of Law, protecting the rights of citizens and defining the parameters of justice. While laws are framed by the Parliament, interpretation is by the judiciary, and there is a substantial body of judge-made law through interpretation of the existing statutes. The Supreme Court of India is headed by the Chief Justice of India who has thirty-three judges on different benches to decide all matters relating to the Constitution of India and the laws formulated under it. The Supreme Court of India has jurisdiction over all disputes between citizens and the Government, both Central and State, as well as all public-sector entities. In addition, it has jurisdiction over any dispute *inter se* between the Central Government and State Governments. The Supreme Court is the final Court of Appeal against any judgment of any High Court, whether in a civil or in a criminal proceeding. The present Indian Judicial system was set up while India was a part of the British Empire. British judge-made law by the Privy Council of the United Kingdom (UK) was persuasive in the initial years after 1947 when India became an independent republic, and by now, the Indian legal system with its body of judge-made laws has almost completely diverged from the laws of the UK other than a few aspects of common law which are still followed. Many of the initial Indian laws were based on British Laws, although the evolution due to amendments and interpretation has been divergent.

5. India has worked on strengthening its intellectual property laws. Today, there is a strong legal structure for protection of intellectual property rights (IPRs). The enforcement remains a challenge, though the courts have been proactive in giving far-reaching judgments to protect IPRs holders.

Chapter 2. Historical Background

6. The Indian sub-continent was historically divided into a number of small kingdoms and principalities, often with a distinct language/dialect, culture, cuisine and cultural identity. With the spread of the Mughal Empire from North India, followed by the British conquest of India, many of these principalities were brought into a single unit, with their rulers executing strategic alliances with the British Indian Government. Following independence in 1947, these principalities were given the choice of acceding to either India or Pakistan and their rights of ownership over privately held land were vested in the Government of India. Approximately 565 princely states merged into India, and approximately 19 went to Pakistan. Indian identity is thus a mosaic of many different cultures and languages. This results in a tremendous amount of diversity.

7. India is, today, the world's largest functioning democracy with approximately 1.44 billion people. It has the seventh largest land mass among countries and is the most populous nation in the world. India is expected to become the third-largest economy in the world by 2027, surpassing Germany and Japan. It is home to one of the most ancient civilizations in the world and has a rich cultural heritage. In the past seventy-seven years, since independence, the country has made significant progress. India is self-sufficient in agricultural production and is now among the top ten industrialized countries in the world and possibly the most populous nation with a relatively young population. India also has significant scientific achievements to its credit, including an active information technology sector and a highly developed space programme.

Part I. Copyright and Neighbouring Rights

Chapter 1. Sources – Legislation

8. The first statute relating to copyright in India was enacted in 1914. It was closely modelled on the UK Copyright Act of 1911. The Act of 1914 was substantively amended and replaced by the Copyright Act of 1957, read with the Copyright Rules of 1958. The legislation that presently governs matters related to copyright in India is the Copyright Act of 1957 (The Act), read with the Copyright Rules of 1958, as amended by the Copyright (Amendment) Act, 2012 and the Copyright Rules, 2013, as amended by the Copyright (Amendment) Rules, 2021.

9. The preamble to the Act states that it is an Act to amend and consolidate the law relating to copyright. Section 16 of the Act specifically states that copyright is a statutory right, and there is, therefore, no common law right in copyright. One cannot claim any copyright beyond the scope of the Act.[1]

10. Efforts to modernize the law in view of changing technology and the international climate continue, and, for this purpose, the law has been amended from time to time, in 1983, 1984, 1992, 1994, 1999, and 2012. The Copyright (Amendment) Act, 1994, was a landmark one, which harmonized the provisions of the Act with the Rome Convention, 1961, by providing protection to the rights of performers, producers of phonograms and broadcasting associations. The Copyright (Amendment) Act of 1999 extended the term for protection of performers' rights from twenty-five years to fifty years, in addition to including in its scope, protection of computer and information technology. The Amendment Act of 1999 inserted a new section 40(A) in the main Act, which empowers the Government to extend the scope of copyright protection to broadcasts and performances made in other countries, provided that these countries extend similar protection to broadcasts and performances made in India. Similarly, by introducing a new section 42(A), the Central Government was empowered to restrict the rights of foreign broadcasters and performers if the country of their origin did not provide protection to Indian broadcasters and performers. These amendments were made to bring the Act in line with the Trade-Related Aspects of Intellectual Property Rights (TRIPS) Agreement, to which India is one of the signatories. The main challenges to the statutory framework are posed by technology, which has opened up many new mechanisms of delivery for

---

1. Entertainment Network (India) Ltd. v. Super Cassette Industries Ltd. & Others (2008) 1 SCC 30; Rediff.com India Ltd. v. E-Eighteen.com Ltd., (2013) 55 PTC 294 (Del).

the same matter. The advent of satellite television has changed the nature of copyright in audio-visual matters as, in addition to overseas rights, there are now also satellite rights and internet rights. Convergence of technology is specially challenging in this context, as many rights are likely to be competing for common delivery mechanisms. Accordingly, various laws have tried to bridge the gap. The Judiciary has been active in protecting copyright through interim relief, although the final determination of claims is a lengthy process.

11. To address the newer issues that have emerged due to digital technology and the Internet, the Ministry of Human Resource Development of India introduced the Copyright (Amendment) Bill, in the beginning of the year 2010. The amendments proposed in the Bill seek to make the provisions of the Copyright Act, 1957 conform to the provisions of the WIPO Copyright Treaty (WCT) and WIPO Performances and Phonograms Treaty (WPPT) which it subsequently acceded to in 2018.[2] The Amendment Bill was passed in 2012 as the Copyright (Amendment) Act, 2012. The provisions provide protection to copyright holders against the circumvention of digital methods applied to protect copyright and provide fines and imprisonment (up to two years) for the circumvention of digital technologies protecting copyright and digital rights management information. Importantly, the Amendment Act provides exclusive rights and moral rights to performers in accordance with WPPT, while it clarifies that authors of literary and musical works, which are included in cinematographic films or sound recordings, receive royalty for the commercial exploitation of such works, Thus, it gives independent rights to authors of literary and musical works in cinematograph films. It also provides for the administration of copyright societies by the owners instead of the producers. It further provides for access to copyright material in specialized formats to physically challenged persons. It also provides for compulsory licensing for certain entities for publication of copyright in other formats, and it has introduced statutory licensing to broadcasting organizations to access literary and musical works. It provides for joint ownership of the copyright in a cinematograph film for the producer and the director of the film and extends the term of the copyright in a photograph to life plus sixty years (from just sixty years at present).[3]

2. Press Information Bureau, News Brief (4 Jul. 2018), https://pib.gov.in/newsite/PrintRelease.aspx?relid=180389.
3. Statement of Object and Reasons of the Copyright (Amendment) Act, 2012.

Chapter 2. Subject Matter of Protection

§1. Different Categories of Protected Works

12. According to section 13(1) of the Act, protected works may be classified under the following three headings:

- original literary, dramatic, musical and artistic works;
- cinematograph films; and
- sound recordings.

13. The conditions subject to which copyright is granted under section 13 are:

- In the case of a published work, the work is first published in India, or where the work is first published outside India, the author is, at the date of such publication, or in a case where the author was dead at that date, was at the time of his death, a citizen of India.
- In the case of an unpublished work other than a work of architecture, the author is, at the date of making such work, a citizen of India or domiciled in India.
- In the case of a work of architecture, if the work is located in India.

14. These conditions, however, do not apply to works that are covered by sections 40 and 41 of the Copyright Act, 1957. Section 40 deals with the powers of the Central Government to extend copyright to foreign works, and section 41 deals with special provisions made for works of certain international organizations. In both these cases, the term of copyright shall not exceed the term of sixty years provided under this Act.

15. The word 'original' has been held to mean that the expression of a thought or an idea should be original, but there is no requirement that the thought or idea itself must be novel or unique. There can be no copyright in a word or words, but only in the manner in which it is written.[4] The Act only requires that the work must originate from the author and not be copied from another work.[5] Any new and original plan, arrangement or compilation of material will entitle the author to copyright therein, whether the materials themselves be old or new. Whoever by his/her own skill, labour and judgment writes a new work may have a copyright therein, unless it is directly copied or evasively imitated from another's work. To secure copyright over the product, it is necessary that the labour, skill and capital expended should be sufficient to impart to the product some quality or character which the original

4. Associated Electronic and Electric Industries, Bangalore Pvt Ltd v. Sharp Tools AIR 1991 Kar 406.
5. Rupendra Kashyap v. Jiwan Publishing House (1996) 16 PTC 439 (Del); Rediff.com India Ltd. v. E-Eighteen.com Ltd., (2013) 55 PTC 294 (Del), which relies on University of London Press v. University of Tutorial Press (1916) 2 Ch. 601.

material did not possess and which differentiates the product from the original material.[6] This is known as the 'doctrine of modicum of creativity', wherein a minimum level of creativity is required to support copyright.[7]

16. Literary Work: The definition under section 2(o) of the Act is an inclusive one, and it states that the term 'literary work' includes computer programs, tables and compilations, including computer databases.

17. Dramatic Work: The Act defines 'dramatic work' under section 2(h) to mean any piece for recitation, choreographic work or entertainment in a dumb show, the scenic arrangement or acting, the form of which is fixed in writing or otherwise, but does not include a cinematograph film.

18. Musical Work: The term is defined in section 2(p) of the Act to mean a work consisting of music and includes any graphical notation of such work but does not include any words or any action intended to be sung, spoken or performed with the music. Musical works and sound recordings embodying the music are separate subjects entitled to independent copyright.

19. Artistic Work: Section 2(c) defines 'artistic work' to mean any work of artistic craftsmanship, including painting, sculpture, drawing (including a diagram, map, chart or plan), engraving, photograph and a work of architecture, whether or not such work possesses artistic quality. In the case of a work of architecture, copyright subsists only in the artistic character and design and does not extend to the processes and methods of construction.[8]

20. Cinematograph Film: The term is defined in the Act, under section 2(f), to mean any work of visuals and includes a sound recording accompanying such visual recording. It is stated further that the term 'cinematograph' shall be construed as including any work produced by any process analogous to cinematography, including video films. Various judicial precedents have outlined that if a separate copyright exists in the screenplay of a cinematographic work, such copyright remains independent and cannot be affected by the copyright held in the cinematographic film.[9]

21. Sound Recording: Section 2(xx) defines the term to mean a recording of sounds from which such sounds may be produced, regardless of the medium on which such recording is made or the method by which the sounds are produced. The

---

6. Macmillan Company Ltd v. K. & J. Cooper AIR 1924 PC 75; Eastern Book Company and Others v. D.B. Modak and Others (101) 2002 DLT 205; Emergent Genetics India Pvt. Ltd. v. Shailendra Shivam and Others (2011) 47 PTC 494 (Del).
7. Syndicate of the Press of the University of Cambridge v. B.D. Bhandari & Another (2011) 47 PTC 244 (Del).
8. Section 13(5).
9. RDB and Co. HUF v. Harpercollins Publishers India Private Limited CS (COMM) 246/2021.

copyright in a sound recording is separate from that which rests in the subject matter of the recording, each of the two works being entitled to their own separate and independent copyright.[10]

§2. Works Excluded from Protection

22. There is no category of work that is specifically excluded from protection under the Act. However, it is clear from various decisions of the courts that copyright does not subsist in thoughts or ideas or in natural or historical events.[11]

23. Copyright is described as subsisting in the 'form' and not in the 'idea'. There is no copyright in ideas.[12] Copyright subsists only in the material form in which the ideas are translated. In *Donoghue v. Allied Newspaper Ltd.*,[13] it was held that *if the idea, however brilliant and however clever it may be, is nothing more than an idea and is not put into any form of words, or any form of expression such as a picture or a play, then there is no such thing as copyright at all. It is not, until it is reduced into writing, or into some tangible form, that you get any right to copyright at all.*[14] In the field of literary work, the words chosen by the author to express his/her ideas are peculiar to him/herself, and no two descriptions of the same idea or fact will be in the same words.[15] The test to distinguish the expression from the idea in a particular work is a legal assessment, arrived at after an in-depth enquiry.[16]

24. Natural or historical events are not copyrightable as such. Ideas, information, natural phenomena and events are common property and cannot be made subject to the copyright of an individual. However, the manner in which the historical or natural event may be depicted or presented may render it copyrightable.[17] In addition, a mere concept cannot be granted copyright protection as was stated in *RG Anand v. M/s. Deluxfilms.*[18] This was reiterated by the Delhi High Court in the case of *Sanjay Gupta v. Sony Pictures Networks India P Ltd.*[19]

25. Another judgment by the Supreme Court in *Eastern Book Company v. D.B. Modak* led to the conclusion that the judicial pronouncements of the Supreme Court

10. Section 13(4).
11. R.G. Anand v. M/s. Deluxfilms and Others AIR 1978 SC 1613; Indian Express Newspaper (Bombay) Pvt. Ltd. v. Jagmohan, AIR 1985 Bom 229.
12. Harnam Pictures N.V. v. Osborne (1967) 1 WLR 723.
13. (1937) 3 Ch.D. 503.
14. Prestige Housewares (India) Limited & Another v. Prestige Estates and Properties & Others (2002) 25 PTC 108 (Karn).
15. Jeffreys v. Boosey (1854) 4 HLC 815 at 868.
16. Institute for Inner Studies & Ors. v. Charlotte Anderson & Ors. (2014) 57 PTC 228 (Del).
17. Indian Express Newspaper Pvt Ltd & Anr v. Dr Jagmohan Mundhara & Ors AIR 1985 Bom 229.
18. Supra n. 10.
19. Sanjay Kumar Gupta & Another v. Sony Pictures Networks India P Ltd. & Others RFA No. 627 of 2018.

are not copyrightable because they are already a part of public domain. Their reproduction and publication do not amount to an infringement of copyright.[20] However, head notes or editorial notes of a judgment are treated as an original literary work and covered under section 13(1)(a) of the Act.[21]

20. Eastern Book Company & Ors v. D.B. Modak & Ors. AIR 2008 SC 809.
21. Infoseek Solutions & Anr. v. Kerala Law Times & Ors. (2007) 34 PTC 231 (Ker).

Chapter 3. Conditions of Protection

§1. Formal Requirements

26. Formal requirements, as conditions, are specified only for two categories of works, that is, sound recordings and cinematographic or video films. For all other categories of works, there are no express formal requirements to be met.

27. Section 52(A) specifically prescribes certain requirements that must be present in sound recordings and video films for them to be copyrightable.

28. In the case of a sound recording, the following particulars have to be mentioned on the sound recording and on any other container thereof:

- the name and address of the person who made the recording;
- the name and address of the Owner of Copyright; and
- the year when the work was first published.

29. In the case of cinematographic or video films, the following details must be displayed before the broadcast of any video film:

- a video film must display the name and address of the owner of the copyright in the film itself while it is being exhibited, as well as carry these particulars on the video cassette or other container of the film;
- if the person who has made the film is not the owner of the copyright in it, then it is additionally necessary for him/her to display, both in the product itself and on its cassette or container, that he/she has obtained the copyright owner's licence or consent for the making of the video film; and
- if the work is a cinematograph film such that it requires a certificate for its exhibition under the provisions of the Cinematograph Act, 1952, then the Copyright Act makes it obligatory that a copy of the certificate granted by the Board of Film Certification be displayed in the film during its exhibition as well as on its container. The Supreme Court has upheld requirements stipulated by certain states, which require video libraries to hold a letter of consent from the holder of the copyright.[22]

As far back as 1999, a report by the National Productivity Council was reflective of the fact that all parties involved in the legitimate transaction of films lost a lot of money owing to widespread video or cable piracy, and this included potential tax revenue lost by the government.[23] The report also highlighted that in the years to come online piracy of content would become another issue. India currently has over nine hundred million internet users by some estimates, with half from rural areas; this figure is increasing as Bharat BroadbandNet is taking the internet to each and

22. South Indian Film Chamber of Commerce v. Entertaining Enterprises (1995) 2 SCC 462.
23. National Productivity Council, Study on Copyright Piracy in India (1999), http://copyright.gov.in/documents/study%20on%20copyright%20piracy%20in%20india.pdf [hereinafter 'N.P.C. Study'].

every village. Earlier, the internet speed was among the lowest in the world.[24] The advent of 3G and 5G have improved services, and while speed and bandwidth are still behind some nations, with the roll out of 6G, the situation is expected to improve further. The rate of adoption of technology in the form of cell phones has been phenomenal, with almost 77% of the 1.44 billion strong population having access to mobile phones.

There have been numerous attempts to address the issue of piracy, such as the Draft Cinematography Bill 2010[25] and recommendations made by a committee headed by Justice Mukul Mudgal.[26] This was followed by another proposed amendment to the Cinematography Act in 2019, to which the Parliamentary Standing Committee on Information Technology recommended a few changes. The Cinematograph (Amendment) Bill, 2023, was further introduced to fight piracy.

Courts have also decided to employ a novel approach to address this problem. For instance, the Delhi High Court in a judgment provided for the use of a dynamic injunction, whereby the plaintiffs were allowed to approach the Joint Registrar of the Delhi High Court to extend an injunction that had already been granted against a website in the event a similar website which contains the same content as the original emerges.[27] This was done by relying on section 7 of the Delhi High Court Act, 1966, read with Chapter II, Rule 3(61), read with Rule 6 of the Delhi High Court (Original Side) Rules 2018. These rules also allow for an aggrieved party to appeal against the joint registrar's orders.

§2. Substantive Requirements

30. The end result of the labour, skill and capital expended by the creator on his/her work is protected by grant of copyright and not the basic elements, thoughts or ideas used in the work. To secure copyright, it is necessary that labour, skill and capital should be expended sufficiently to impart to the product some quality or character which the basic material did not possess and which differentiates the product from the basic material.[28] The amount of knowledge, labour, judgment, literary skill or taste, which the creator must bestow upon his/her creation in order to acquire copyright, cannot be defined in precise terms. It would depend upon the facts of each case.

---

24. Deloitte Broadband: The Lifeline of Digital India (2014), https://www2.deloitte.com/content/dam/Deloitte/in/Documents/technology-media-telecommunications/in-tmt-broadband-noexp.pdf.
25. The Cinematograph (Amendment) Bill, 2010 – http://164.100.47.4/billstexts/lsbilltexts/asintroduced/2651ls.pdf.
26. Report of the Committee of Experts to Examine Issues of Certification under the Cinematograph Act 1952, 28 Sep. 2013 – https://mib.gov.in/sites/default/files/Report_of_Expert_committee.pdf, https://www.pib.gov.in/newsite/PrintRelease.aspx?relid=100173.
27. UTV Software Communication Ltd. & Ors. v. 1337X.TO & Ors. CS (COMM) 724/2017 & ors.
28. Macmillan Company Ltd v. K. & J. Cooper AIR 1924 PC 75; Eastern Book Company and Other v. D.B. Modak and Others (101) 2002 DLT 205.

Chapter 4. Ownership

§1. The Author

31. The definition of 'author' as given under section 2(d) states that an author means:

- in relation to a literary or dramatic work, the author of that work;
- in relation to a musical work, the composer (it may be noted that while copyright in the music belongs to the composer, the copyright in a recording made of the music vests in the producer of the recording and not in the original composer);
- in relation to an artistic work other than a photograph, the artist;
- in relation to a photograph, the person who took the photograph;
- in relation to a cinematographic film or sound recording, the producer;
- in relation to an architectural work or other work involving artistic craftsmanship, the architect or artist, as the case may be; and
- in relation to a literary, dramatic, musical or artistic work that is computer-generated, it is the person who causes the work to be created.

32. As per section 17, the author of a work shall be the first owner of copyright subject to other provisions of the Act. However, where the work of the author has been commissioned by any other person, then in the absence of any agreements to the contrary, such other person shall be the owner of the copyright in the work as it constitutes a work made for hire.[29] The Copyright Act, 1957, as amended in 2012, vide section 13(1)(a) provides that copyright subsists in original literary, dramatic, musical and artistic works, cinematograph films and sound recording. The proviso to section 17(e) states that in case of any work incorporated in a cinematograph work, the fact that the work has been commissioned will not affect the right of the author therein under the Act. In the context of Cinematographic Work, the 'contract of service' under clause (c) to the provisio of section 17 of the Act does not apply explicitly to cases of a contract between equals (like the one between the producers); instead, it is to be interpreted as an employment contract between master and servant.

§2. Joint Ownership

33. The Act, under section 2(z), defines a work of joint authorship to mean a work produced by the collaboration of two or more authors in which the contribution of one author is not distinct from the contribution of the other author or authors. In the case of joint authorship in a copyrightable work, each of the joint authors may claim ownership which vests collectively in them and not in any one of them individually.

---

29. Proviso (b) and (c) to s. 17, see also Diljeet Titus Advocate & Others v. Alfred A. Adebare & Others (2006) 32 PTC 609 (Del).

34. If there is an intellectual contribution by two or more persons, pursuant to a pre-concerted joint design to the composition of a literary work, then those persons who have contributed to the work have to be regarded as joint authors.[30] There are three ingredients for a work to be called a work of joint authorship, i.e., collaboration, non-distinction of the contribution from one another and creative input.[31]

35. Furthermore, in the event of Joint Ownership of Copyright, the High Court of Bombay in *Angath Arts Private Limited v. Century Communications Ltd.*[32] held that the joint owner of a copyright cannot, without the consent of the other joint owner, grant a licence or interest in the copyright to a third party.

36. As per Indian Jurisprudence, the joint owners of a copyright cannot exploit the copyright individually; they can only do so jointly. Thus, no joint owner can assign, transfer, licence or sublicence in any other manner using the copyright without the concurrence of the other joint owners.

§3. Works Made for Hire

37. The courts have held that the artistic work of an author made as an employee, and while in the course of employment, passes on to the employer in contingencies specified in section 17(c).[33] However, in the event there exists a dispute regarding the ownership of copyright being between an employer and an employee, the Delhi High Court's judgment in the matter of *Neetu Singh v. Rajiv Saumitra*[34] clarifies that it is the *terms of employment* of the employee that have to be looked into.

38. As per the above-stated parameter, it is essential to determine whether the work was created by the employee as part of the terms of employment, in order for the employer to claim ownership of that work. This case also states the aspects that need to be examined to determine the terms of employment, such as in the case of a Director, it would be the Articles of Association/Memorandum of Association of the company or any other subsisting agreement. This decision may also be applied to other forms of employment by simply looking at any agreement between an employer and an employee.

39. In the case of a musical work, the first owner is the composer of the work, except where the work was composed in the course of employment under a contract of service. However, in the case of contract for service, the copyright vests with the composer.[35]

---

30. Najma Heptulla v. Orient Longman Ltd and Others AIR 1989 Del 63.
31. Institute for Inner Studies & Ors. v. Charlotte Anderson & Ors. (2014) 57 PTC 228 (Del).
32. Angath Arts Private Limited v. Century Communications Ltd. and Anr. 2008 (4) Mh.L.J. 926.
33. V.T. Thomas and Ors v. Malayala Manorama Co Ltd AIR 1989 Ker 49.
34. Neetu Singh v. Rajiv Saumitra & Ors. CS(COMM) 935/2016.
35. Gee Pee Film Pvt Ltd. v. Pratik Chowdhury & Ors. (2002) 24 PTC 392 (Cal).

40. Where the employer is a government department, then, in the absence of any agreement to the contrary, it is the government that is the first owner of the copyright. This is also true of works made or commissioned by a public-sector undertaking or international organizations or agencies.[36]

36. Sections 17(d), (dd) and (e).

Chapter 5. Transfer

§1. Assignments of Copyright

41. An assignment of copyright under section 18 of the Act may be with or without any limitations, the terms of which are usually set out in an agreement between the parties. Copyright may be assigned in respect of future works of an author, that is, before the work comes into existence, but in such a case, the assignment takes effect only when the work comes into existence. After 2012, major changes have been made in the scope of assignment under section 18. Proviso (2) to section 18 states that no assignment can be applied to any medium or mode of exploitation, which did not exist or was not in commercial use at the time of assignment, unless the assignment specifically referred to such medium or mode of exploitation. Proviso (3) to section 18 further provides that the authors of literary or musical work included in a cinematograph film shall not assign or waive their right to receive royalties. They can share these rights on an equal basis with an assignee of copyright for utilization in any form other than for communication to the public in a cinema hall. Authors can assign their right to receive royalty to the legal heirs of the authors or to a copyright society. Proviso (4) further states that the authors of a literary/musical work included in the sound recording (not forming part of a cinematographic film) shall not assign or waive their right to receive royalties. They can share these rights on an equal basis with an assignee of copyright for utilization in any form other than for communication to the public in a cinema hall. Authors can assign their right to receive royalty to the legal heirs of the authors or to a copyright society.

In effect, these changes mean that even if the author of a literary or musical work has assigned his/her copyright in the work to be included in a cinematograph film or a sound recording, he/she shall still receive royalties to be shared on an equal basis with the producers of the film or sound recording. Any agreement/assignment to the contrary shall be void.

42. Section 19 states that no assignment is valid unless it is in writing[37] and is signed by the assignor or by his/her duly authorized agent. An oral assignment of copyright is neither permissible nor valid.[38] It is also mandatory for the agreement to include the following information:

- the identity of the work;
- the particular rights assigned;
- the period for which the work is assigned;
- the territory for which it is assigned; and
- the amount of royalty payment to be made to the author or his/her legal heirs during the period of the assignment.

37. Gramaphone Company of India v. Shanti Films Corporation and Others AIR 1997 Cal 63 at 76.
38. K.A. Venugopal Setty v. Dr Suryakanta U. Kamath AIR 1992 Kar 1.

43. Though no particular form of assignment is prescribed in the Act, the only requirement is that it must be in writing and must be signed by the assignor or his/her authorized agent.[39]

Where the assignee fails to exercise his/her rights under the assignment within a year, his/her rights will be deemed to have lapsed, unless otherwise provided for in the assignment terms. If the assignment is silent about the term of the assignment, it will be deemed to be for a period of five years from the date of assignment. In case the geographical extent of the assignment is not specified, the territory of the assignment will be presumed to be limited to India. These conditions specified in section 19(4), (5), and (6) are not applicable to assignments made prior to the coming into force of the Copyright (Amendment) Act, 1994.[40]

44. Copyright may be transferred upon death by operation of law or through a testamentary disposition. Where an artistic work has been bequeathed to a beneficiary without specifically bequeathing the copyright in it, the law presumes that in the absence of a contrary intention appearing in the will itself, the bequest has been made with the copyright attached to it.

The Copyright (Amendment) Act, 2012, added three more provisions to section 19, whereby the right of the author to receive royalties from the utilization of the work being part of a cinematograph film or sound recordings is protected.[41] Section 19(8) provides that any assignment of copyright in any work shall be void if it is contrary to the terms and conditions of rights already assigned to a copyright society in which the author is a member.[42]

45. Section 19(A) provides that disputes arising with regard to assignment, for instance, where the assignee has failed to exercise or make sufficient use of the assigned rights, would be dealt with in the first instance by the Copyright Board instituted under the Act. Section 19(A) also prescribes the procedure with regard to complaints arising in assignment disputes and vests the Board with powers to revoke the assignment in specified circumstances. It further provides that the Copyright Board shall deal with every complaint as far as possible and try to pass the final order within a period of six months from the date of receipt of complaint, and in case of any delay, the Board shall record the reasons for the same.[43]

46. Section 20 of the Act provides for instances in which the creator of a work passes away before the publication of the work; in such cases, copyright can be transferred as per the deceased's will, ensuring protection and potential publication.

47. Section 21 of the Act provides for instances where the author of a work relinquishes all or any of the rights that constitute his/her copyright. If he/she does so,

---

39. Rupendra Kashyap v. Jiwan Publishing House (1996) 16 PTC 439 (Del); Shemaroo Entertainment Ltd. v. Amrit Sharma and Ors. (2012) 52 PTC 325 (Del); Dorling Kindersley (India) Pvt. Ltd. v. Sanguine Technical Publishers & Ors. (2013) 56 PTC 40 (Del).
40. Section 19(7).
41. Section 19(9) and (10).
42. Section 19(8).
43. The Copyright (Amendment) Act, 2012.

the author must give notice in the prescribed form (Form 1) to the Registrar of Copyrights, who will, within fourteen days from the publication of the notice in the Official Gazette, post the notice on their website. Such notice will remain posted for a period of at least three years, whereupon the copyright as has been relinquished will cease to exist, with effect from the date of the notice. In effect, upon relinquishment, the work falls within the public domain, and any person can use the same without requiring any assignment or licence.

§2. Licences

48. Section 19 of the Act has been made applicable, *mutatis mutandis*, to the provisions for licensing of copyright under section 30, as per the provisions of section 30(A). Therefore, an agreement purporting to create a licensing of copyright, other than in writing, would be neither valid nor permissible under the Act. Although no specific form is prescribed for a licence agreement, the grant of a licence must be in writing, signed by the copyright owner or by his/her authorized agent.[44] As with assignments, a licence may be granted in an existing or future work, and the grant may be for any interest in the whole or part of the rights.[45] In the case of a future work, the licence takes effect only after the work comes into existence. Where the copyright owner of a future work dies before the licence comes into effect, the right to claim the benefit vests in his/her legal representatives unless the agreement provides otherwise. The requirements as to the details to be included in an agreement to grant a licence and consequences of non-use of such licence are also the same as in the assignment of copyright.[46]

There is a distinction between assignment and licence. An assignment transfers title in the copyright; a licence merely permits certain things to be done by the licensee.[47]

49. Provisions for compulsory licences to be granted in works that are withheld from the public are dealt with under section 31. The section now provides that the owner of a copyright and an applicant should be given a reasonable opportunity of being heard by the Commercial Courts and the IPD division since the Intellectual Property Appellate Board (IPAB) and the Copyright Board before it have been disbanded post the promulgation of the Tribunal Ordinance 2021.[48] After holding such an enquiry, if the court is satisfied that the refusal of the owner of a copyright to publish or perform his/her work is unreasonable, it may direct the Registrar of

44. Leopold Café & Stores & Anr. v. Novex Communication Pvt. Ltd. (2014) 59 PTC 505 (Bom).
45. Wallington Cinema Co v. Performing Rights Society Ltd AIR 1937 Bom 472.
46. Section 30(A) read with s. 19(A) of the Act.
47. Deshmukh & Co. (Publishers) Pvt. Ltd. v. Avinasj Vishnu Khandekar & Ors. (2006) 32 PTC 358 (Bom).
48. Tribunal Reforms (Rationalisation and Conditions of Service) Ordinance 2021. For the purpose of the Copyright Act, the term 'Commercial Court' refers to the Commercial Court constituted under s. 3, or the Commercial Division of a High Court constituted under s. 4, of the Commercial Courts Act, 2015.

Copyrights to grant a compulsory licence to such person or persons who in the opinion of the court is or are qualified to do so, to publish, perform, or communicate the work to the public. Rule 6 of the Copyright Rules, 2013, specifies the prescribed manner of application under section 31. In granting a compulsory licence, the court must strike a balance between the rights of the owner of a copyright and the applicants' right to get a compulsory licence.[49] Thus, while deciding the application for a compulsory licence, the court must consider the following: the work has been published or performed in public; wilful refusal of the owner of the copyright/sound recordings to republish or perform the work in public, thereby withholding the work from public; and refusal of the owner of the copyright to communicate the work in public by a broadcasting organization on reasonable terms.[50]

Circumstances under which a compulsory licence may be granted in unpublished Indian works or any work published or communicated to the public and the work is withheld from the public in India are set out in section 31(A). Section 31B provides for compulsory licence for the benefit of disabled persons. Under section 31B, any person working for the benefit of persons with disability on a profit basis or for business may apply in the prescribed manner to the Commercial Court for a compulsory licence to publish any work in which copyright subsists for the benefit of such persons, provided section 52(1)(zb) does not apply. The court shall dispose of the application within two months from the date of application, after an enquiry into the credentials of the applicant and being satisfied that the application has been made in good faith. The licence issued under this section shall specify the period within which such work shall be published, the medium and format in which it shall be published, and the number of copies to be produced. It will also specify the rate at which royalties shall be paid to the owner of the copyright and the person to whom such royalties are to be paid.[51] In case an extension is required, the court may extend the period of compulsory licence after an enquiry upon an application.[52] This is also in accordance with the Marrakesh Treaty to Facilitate Access to Published Works for Persons Who are Blind, Visually Impaired or Otherwise Print Disabled, 2013. The treaty seeks to improve access for the blind, visually impaired and print disabled by publishing works in disabled-friendly formats like Braille, large print text or audio books, which India ratified in July 2014.

Section 31C provides for statutory licensing for cover versions. Prior to 2012, the cover version was allowed under section 52(1)(j)[53] under 'permitted use'. Under section 31C, any person wanting to make a cover version, i.e., a sound recording in respect of any literary, dramatic or musical work, where sound recordings have been made by the licence or with the consent of the owner, can do so, after satisfying the conditions specified therein. The cover version has to be made in the same medium as the last recording unless the said medium is no longer in commercial use. Thus, a sound recording includes a cover version recording.[54] Rules 23–28 prescribe the

---

49. Entertainment Network (India) Ltd v. Super Cassette Industries Ltd (2008) 13 SCC 30; Phonographic Performance Ltd. v. Music Broadcast Pvt. Ltd. and Ors. (2004) 29 PTC 282 (Bom).
50. Entertainment Network (India) Ltd v. Super Cassette Industries Ltd (2008) 13 SCC 30.
51. Section 31(B)(4) read with Rule 18.
52. Proviso to s. 31(B)(4).
53. Repealed under the Copyright (Amendment) Act, 2012.
54. Star India Pvt. Ltd. v. Piyush Agarwal & Ors. (2014) 58 PTC 169 (Del).

manner and format for making cover versions, including notice for making cover version, conditions to be followed, notice for making additional copies, maintenance of records, and manner of determining royalties, among others.

Section 31D provides for statutory licence for broadcasting of literary and musical works and sound recording. As per section 31D, any broadcasting organization, which is desirous of communicating to the public by way of a broadcast or by way of performance of a literary or musical work and sound recording already published can do so, subject to the conditions specified therein. The broadcasting organization has to give prior notice of its intention to broadcast the work specifying the duration and territorial coverage of the broadcast. Nothing in section 31D shall affect the operation of any licence issued or agreement entered into force prior to the commencement of the Copyright (Amendment) Act, 2012.[55] Rules 29–31 of the Copyright Rules, 2013 prescribe the manner and format for obtaining statutory licence for broadcasting of literary and musical works and sound recordings.

A decision by a single judge bench of the Bombay High Court has generated a fair bit of debate regarding the contours of compulsory licensing under the Copyrights Act. In *Tips Industries Ltd. v. Wynk Music Ltd.*, it was held that Wynk's (an online streaming service) feature of allowing users to download songs and store for unlimited future use constituted 'sale' and not 'communication to the public', and therefore, did not constitute a 'broadcast' for the purpose of section 31D.[56] Therefore, Wynk cannot claim a statutory licence for the use of such works.

This decision is in appeal before a division bench of the Bombay High Court, and there appears to be recognition from the government's end that to end all confusion, internet or digital broadcasters should be included in the definition of Compulsory Licensing within section 31D.[57]

Section 32 deals with the granting of a licence to produce and publish translations, and section 32(A) sets out provisions for the grant of a licence to reproduce and publish works for certain purposes. Provisions for the termination of a licence issued under the Act are dealt with under section 32(B).

55. Section 31D(8).
56. Tips Industries Ltd. v. Wynk Music Ltd. & Anr. Commercial IP Suit (L) No. 114 of 2018.
57. Parliament of India, Rajya Sabha, Department Related Parliamentary Standing Committee on Commerce, Review of the Intellectual Property Rights Regime in India, 161st Report (23 Jul. 2021) https://rajyasabha.nic.in/rsnew/Committee_site/Committee_File/ReportFile/13/141/161_2021_7_15.pdf.

Chapter 6. Scope of the Exclusive Rights

§1. Moral Rights

50. Apart from economic rights conferred by the Act, the author of a work also has certain moral rights, which are recognized by the general law of the land in all civilized countries.[58] These are:

(1) the right to decide whether to publish or not to publish the work (*droit de divulgation* – the right of publication);
(2) the right to claim authorship of a published or exhibited work (*droit a la paternite* – the right of paternity); and
(3) the right to prevent alteration and other actions that may damage the author's honour or reputation (*droit au respect de loeuvre* – the right of integrity).

The Berne Convention (Article 6) recognizes some of these rights and requires Member States to provide the author with the right to claim authorship and to object to alterations. These rights remain with the author even after the transfer of copyright, and the protection lasts during the whole of the copyright term. The author's moral rights are independent of his/her economic rights. The author has a right to preserve, protect and nurture his/her creations through his/her moral rights.[59] If the author intends to transfer the moral rights also, he/she should state so specifically in writing in the deed of assignment.[60] However, after the Delhi High Court's decision in the *Amar Nath Sehgal* case, it appears that these rights cannot be waived off.[61]

51. There is no reference in the Act to 'moral rights' as such. However, section 57 provides for certain special rights of authors that are independent of copyright and remain with the author even after the assignment of copyright. Under this special concept, the artist enjoys a right to ensure that the integrity of his/her work is not violated or distorted by someone who derives the right of adaptation, translation, etc. These rights are in addition to those available to the owners of general copyright. It is based on the principle that damage to the reputation of the author is independently actionable, separate from the infringement of the work itself.

52. Various judicial decisions have affirmed that an author, under this special provision, has the exclusive right to authorize any derivative work based on his/her work and also to exercise the corresponding right of preventing through an injunction, unauthorized adaptations or adaptations that go beyond what was authorized.[62]

58. See International Copyright by Steward, 7.
59. Amar Nath Sehgal v. Union of India (2005) 30 PTC 253 (Del).
60. International Copyright by Stewart, 61.
61. Supra n. 60.
62. Mannu Bhandari v. Kala Vikas Pictures Pvt Ltd and another AIR 1987 Del 13; Amar Nath Sehgal v. Union of India (2005) 30 PTC 253 (Del).

Even in cases of assignment of copyright, the author can approach the court to protect him/her from serious injury or distortion of work.[63]

53. The following are the author's special rights under section 57 of the Act:

- to claim authorship of the work; and
- to restrain or claim damages in respect of any distortion, mutilation, modification or other act in relation to the work if such distortion, mutilation, modification or other act would be prejudicial to his/her honour or reputation. This right may also be claimed by the legal representatives of the author.

54. However, failure to display the work, or display the work to the satisfaction of the author, will not be deemed to be an infringement of the aforesaid rights. Further, in case of any adaptation of a computer program to which section 52(1)(aa) applies, the author does not have the right to restrain or claim damages.

55. Evidence may be necessary to establish the allegation of distortion, mutilation or other modification amounting to violation of the author's right under section 57.[64]

56. A recent judgment by the Delhi High Court added another layer to jurisprudence concerning moral rights. The court in *RajRewal v. UOI* held that an architect as the creator and legal author of a building having artistic significance cannot use his moral rights as a basis to supersede the rights of the building owner to destroy or modify the building.[65] This judgment, if interpreted expansively, does appear to run counter to the opinion of the Delhi High Court in the *Amarnath Sehgal* case.[66] In the former case, the Hon'ble Court held that the destruction of a work does not constitute a violation of rights under section 57 which also restricts the scope of moral rights to those codified under the copyright itself. However, in the latter case, the Hon'ble Court has relied upon international conventions to make a case for preservation of cultural heritage while interpreting section 57.

57. Though a distinction needs to be made between the two cases, the former case entailed an architectural work while the latter concerned a work of art. It will be interesting to witness if courts in future use the nature of the object to determine the degree of moral rights that an 'author' can lay access to in their creation.

58. The author's moral or special rights can be enforced under other branches of law – e.g., under the law of defamation if the author's reputation is damaged, under the law of contract for breach of the implied term of contract or breach of trust if any person publishes the work without the author's consent and under the law of

---

63. Arun Chadha v. OCA Productions Private Limited (2013).
64. Garapati Prasad Rao v. Parmandi Saroja AIR 1992 AP 230.
65. RajRewal v. Union of India & Ors. CS(COMM) No. 3/2018.
66. Divij Joshi, Delhi High Court Rules That Moral Rights Offer No Remedy for Destruction of a Work, SPICY IP (31 May 2019) https://spicyip.com/2019/05/delhi-high-court-rules-that-moral-rights-offer-no-remedy-for-destruction-of-a-work.html.

passing off where some person has misled the public into the belief that he/she is the author of the work. Section 57 gives statutory recognition to moral rights that were recognized under common law.[67]

§2. Exploitation Rights

59. The rights that an author of a work is entitled to under the Act are defined in section 14. These rights are, however, subject to the other provisions of the Act. These rights are to do or authorize the doing of any of the following acts in respect of a work or any substantial part thereof.

60. In the case of a literary, dramatic or musical work, not being a computer program:

- to produce the work in any material form, including the storing of it in any medium by electronic means;
- to issue copies of the work to the public not being copies already in circulation;
- to perform the work in public or communicate it to the public;
- to make any cinematograph film or sound recording in respect of the work;
- to make any translation of the work;
- to make any adaptation of the work; and
- to do, in relation to a translation or adaptation of the work, any of the acts specified above.

These rights are subject to the conditions of assignment and licence, as specified in the Act.

61. In the case of a computer program:

- to do any of the acts specified in relation to a literary work; and
- to sell or give on commercial rental, or offer for sale or for commercial rental, any copy of the computer program, provided that such commercial rental does not apply in respect of computer programs, where the program itself is not the essential object of the rental.

62. In the case of an artistic work:

- to reproduce the work in any material form, including the storing of it in any medium by electronic or other means; or depiction in three dimensions of a two-dimensional work; or depiction in two-dimensions of a two-dimensional work;
- to communicate the work to the public;
- to issue copies of the work to the public not being copies already in circulation;
- to include the work in any cinematograph film;
- to make any adaptation of the work; and

67. P. Narayanan's Intellectual Property Law. Eastern Law House (1997).

- to do in relation to an adaptation of the work any of the acts specified in relation to the above.

63. In the case of a cinematograph film:

- to make a copy of the film, including a photograph of any image forming part thereof; or storing it in any medium by electronic or other means;
- to sell or give on commercial rental or offer for sale or for such rental any copy of the film; and
- to communicate the film to the public.

64. In the case of a sound recording:

- to make any other sound recording embodying it, including storing it in any medium by electronic or other means; and
- to sell or give on commercial rental or offer for sale or for such rental any copy of the sound recording.

65. Broadcasting Rights: As per the provisions of section 37, every broadcasting organization has a special right known as a 'broadcast reproduction right' in respect of its broadcasts. This right will subsist for twenty-five years from the year following that in which the broadcast is first made. During this period, if any person does the following acts without a licence from the owner of the broadcasting right, that person will be deemed to have infringed the broadcast reproduction rights:

- re-broadcasts the broadcast;
- causes the broadcast to be heard or seen by the public on payment of any charges;
- makes any sound recording or visual recording of the broadcast; or
- makes any reproduction of such sound recording or visual recording where such initial recording was done without licence or where it was licensed, for any purpose not envisaged by such licence; or
- sells or gives on commercial rental or offer for sale or for such rental, any such sound recording or visual recording referred above.

66. However, under section 39, certain acts will not amount to infringement of broadcast reproduction rights. These acts are:

- the making of any sound recording or visual recording for the private use of the person making such recording or solely for purposes of bona fide teaching or research; or
- the use, consistent with fair dealing, of excerpts of a broadcast in the reporting of current events or for bona fide review, teaching or research; or
- such other acts, with necessary adaptation and modifications, which do not constitute infringement of copyright under section 52.

67. A programme broadcast usually includes literary, dramatic or musical works or records in which independent copyright may subsist. In such cases, the broadcasting organization should obtain the consent or licence of the copyright owners in the work in question because copyright in such works includes the right to communicate the work to the public.[68]

68. The broadcast reproduction right does not affect the copyright in any literary, dramatic or musical work, which is broadcast or in any recording any such work. After the 2012 amendment, the rights of the authors of original literary, dramatic, musical or artistic works which are incorporated in cinematograph films shall still persist. Further, the author of a lyric or a musical work retains the right of performing it in public for profit, otherwise than as part of a cinematograph film.[69]

The jurisprudence on the interplay between section 2(ff) and section 14 and its various sub-sections have generated interesting points of law. One such case was the Madras High Court adjudication in *Thiagarajan Kumararaja v. M/s Capital Film Works.*[70] Herein, the two key questions were whether the dubbing of a film and the remaking of a film came within the definition of 2(ff). The court held in the affirmative for the former and the negative for the latter.

The reasoning was that the term 'communication to the public' needs to be read expansively along with the fact that a producer's right to communicate the film to the public through dubbing does not affect the rights of the author of the underlying script. Remaking a film would be an abrogation of this principle under section 2(ff) as it would entail making changes to the underlying script without the author's consent, thus infringing the author's exclusive rights.

---

68. Section 14(a)(iii), (c)(ii), (d), (e)(iii) and s. 2(ff).
69. Music Broadcast Private Limited v. Indian Performing Right Society (2011) 47 PTC 587 (Bom).
70. Thiagarajan Kumararaja v. M/s Capital Film Works and Anr. OS(App.) No. 22 of 2017.

Chapter 7. Limitations or Exemptions to the Scope of Copyright Protection

69. Section 52 lists certain acts that are not to be considered as infringing copyright in any work. It provides that a fair dealing with a literary, dramatic, musical, or artistic work for the following purposes does not constitute infringement: research or private study, criticism or review, whether of that work or of any other work, reporting current events and current affairs, including the reporting of a lecture delivered in public. In the case of criticism or review or newspaper reporting, it must be accompanied by an acknowledgement identifying the work by its title or other description and identifying the author. The Act allows the use of literary, dramatic, musical or artistic works, which is required for the reporting of current events, and not more.[71]

70. The above provisions also apply to the translation of a literary, dramatic or musical work or the adaptation of a literary, dramatic, musical or artistic work, as they apply in relation to the work itself. Under section 52 of the Copyright Act, 1957, fair dealing covers translation or adaptation of a literary, dramatic, musical or artistic work for the purpose of private use, which includes criticism, review and research.[72] The principles of fair dealing have been clearly enunciated by the Delhi High Court in *Super Cassettes Industries Ltd. v. Hamar Television Network Pvt. Ltd. & Another.*[73]

When discussing section 52, it would be pertinent to take note of the DU Photocopy case and the Delhi High Court's historic pronouncement regarding the same. Justice Rajiv Sahai Endlaw dismissed the suit filed by three publishers against DU and a photocopy shop by holding that unauthorized making and distribution of course packs does not amount to copyright infringement as it falls within the ambit of section 52(1)(i) of the Copyright Act that permits reproduction of works by teachers or students in the course of instruction.[74] On appeal, the Division Bench interpreted section 52(1)(i) as permitting photocopying of copyrighted works for preparation of course packs, irrespective of the quantity, as long as it is for the purpose of educational instruction.[75] Accordingly, the suit was remanded for a factual determination on the purpose of works photocopied in this case.

71. In an action for infringement of copyright, if the defendant pleads fair dealing, an interlocutory injunction may not be granted.[76] The various other acts that are

71. Super Cassettes Industries Limited v. Chintamani Rao & Others (2012) 49 PTC 1 (Del); New Delhi Television Limited v. ICC Development (International) Ltd. & Anr. (2013) 53 PTC 71 (Del).
72. Academy of General Education, Manipal and Anr v. B. Malini Mallya (AIR 2009 SC 1982).
73. (2011) 45 PTC 70 (Del).
74. The Chancellor, Masters & Scholars of the University of Oxford & Ors. v. Rameshwari Photocopy Services & Anr. CS(OS) 2439/2012.
75. The Chancellor, Masters & Scholars of the University of Oxford & Ors. v. Rameshwari Photocopy Services & Anr. RFA(OS) 81/2016.
76. Hubbard v. Vosper (1972) 2 QB 84; (1972) 1 All ER 1023 CA; Fraser v. Evans (1969) 1 QB 349; (1969) 1 All ER 8 CA; Pepsico Inc and Anr. v. Hindustan Coca cola and Ors 94 (2001) DLT 30.

exempted under section 52 include the reproduction of any literary, dramatic, musical, or artistic work for judicial proceedings, for teaching purposes, the reading in public of any reasonable extract from any published work, performance given to a non-paying audience or for the benefit of a religious institution, the adaptation, reproduction, issue of copies or communication to the public in any accessible format for persons with disability, etc.

72. The main challenges to the system of copyright protection are likely to arise from the convergence of technology. The Information Technology Act, 2000, provides for legal recognition of transactions carried out by means of electronic data, and this has far-reaching implications for both copyright and trademark protection. The emergence of a common delivery mechanism is likely to spawn litigation over the nature of rights in the broadcast media and literary media. The Copyright (Amendment) Act, 1999, excludes from the scope of protection any information essential for interoperability of computer programs, ideas and principles which underline any elements of a program and the making of copies or adaptation of computer programs for non-commercial personal use. The objective is to enable research and development. Similarly, the Copyright (Amendment) Act, 2012, further clarified this aspect. It provided that storing of any work in any electronic medium for the purposes of personal use or research, criticism or review, reporting of current events and affairs, including the incidental storage of any computer program, which is not in itself an infringing copy for the said purposes, shall not constitute infringement of copyright. It further exempts the storing of a work in any medium by electronic means by a non-commercial public library for preservation if the library already possesses a non-digital copy of the work.

73. Legal issues arising out of information technology, compounded with the convergence of technology, are just beginning to surface in India, and more clarity is required on the direction that protection of data transmitted by these means will take place. It was a similar set of questions that were dealt with by the Delhi High Court in the *My Space v. T-series* case.[77] The court on the question of intermediary liability held that intermediaries are immune from liability against secondary copyright infringement for third-party content unless '*actual knowledge*' on their part can be proved and if the entity does not fail to expeditiously take down content upon receiving such knowledge. The Bench, while arriving at the decision, has ruled that section 79 of the Information Technology Act, 2000 ('*IT Act*'), provides a 'safe harbour' to intermediaries and the same is not struck by the proviso to section 81 of the same Act in case of copyright infringement actions. In its understanding of actual knowledge, the court in this instance interpreted differently than the Supreme Court in *Shreya Singhal v. Union of India*, which stated that a court order or, on being notified by the appropriate government, directing removal of certain content

77. My Space Inc. v. Super Cassettes Industries Ltd. FAO (OS) 540/2011.

would serve as actual notice.[78] The reason for this differentiation could be attributed to the Supreme Court focusing on the restrictions present under Article 19(2) of the Constitution.[79]

74. In the period since the *My Space* judgment, a few legal contestations involving both copyright and trademarks have expanded the discussion on Intermediary Liability and the means to address it.

75. To start with, the Delhi High Court in *Christian Louboutin Sas v. Nakul Bajaj* stated that the intermediary must be an active participant in the alleged infringement or illegal act for the standard for 'conspiring, aiding, abetting or inducing' to be met.[80] This is the standard used for determining if the entity in question is going to be liable for secondary infringement under the Copyright Act. Courts have also used the responsibilities of an intermediary with respect to availing safe harbour to impose global blocking order, as was done by the Delhi High Court in *Swami Ramdev v. Facebook Inc.*[81]

76. While the *My Space* decision was rightly heralded, the domain of intermediary liability in situations involving Copyright and Trademark infringement is still evolving. The new IT Rules 2021 have created new categories such as Social Media Intermediaries and Significant Social Media Intermediaries (SMI & SSMI) with differing levels of accountability.[82] It would be interesting to witness how the law evolves given these new regulations.

---

78. Shreya Singhal v. Union of India WP (CrL.) No. 167 of 2012.
79. Article 19(2) of the Constitution of India, 1947.
80. Christian Louboutin Sas v. Nakul Bajaj CS (COMM) 344/2018.
81. Swami Ramdev & Anr. v. Facebook Inc. & Ors. CS (OS) 27/2019 – I.A. 855/2019.
82. Information Technology (Intermediary Guidelines and Digital Media Ethics Code) Rules, 2021 – https://mib.gov.in/sites/default/files/IT%28Intermediary%20Guidelines%20and%20Digital%20Media%20Ethics%20Code%29%20Rules%2C%202021%20English.pdf.

Chapter 8. Duration of Protection

77. The Act deals with the term of copyright for different categories of works that are granted protection in sections 22–29.

§1. Literary, Dramatic, Musical or Artistic Work

78. When a work is published within the lifetime of the author, copyright subsists during the lifetime of the author and until sixty years from the beginning of the calendar year following the year in which the author dies. Where the work is of joint authorship, the sixty-year period will commence after the death of the author who dies last (section 22).

§2. Anonymous or Pseudonymous Works

79. In the case of anonymous or pseudonymous works, the term of copyright is until sixty years from the beginning of the calendar year following the year in which the work is first published. If the identity of the author is disclosed before the expiry of the said period, copyright subsists until sixty years from the beginning of the calendar year following the year in which the author dies. In the case of an anonymous work of joint authorship where the identity of one of the authors is disclosed, the sixty-year period is to be counted as above after the death of that author. Where the identity of more than one author is disclosed, the sixty-year period will start, as above, after the death of the author who dies last (section 23).

§3. Posthumous Work

80. In the case of literary, dramatic or musical works or engravings where copyright subsists at the date of death of the author who dies last and the work or an adaptation of which has not been published before that date, copyright will subsist until sixty years from the beginning of the calendar year following the year in which the work is first published. Where an adaptation of the work is published in any earlier year, the sixty-year period will commence from the calendar year following that year. For the purpose of the above, a literary, dramatic or musical work or an adaptation of any such work is deemed to be published if it has been performed in public or if any sound recording made in respect of the work has been sold to the public or have been offered for sale to the public (section 24).

§4. Cinematographic Film

81. Copyright subsists until sixty years from the beginning of the calendar year following the year in which the film is published (section 26). Furthermore, the

Madras High Court also clarified that this is a non-derogable provision; that is, even if parties enter into a contract restricting the term of copyright protection, it will not be allowed to persist.[83]

§5. Sound Recording

82. Copyright subsists until sixty years from the beginning of the calendar year following the year in which the record is published (section 27).

§6. Government Work

83. Where the Government is the first owner of the copyright, copyright will subsist until sixty years from the beginning of the calendar year following the year in which the work is first published (section 28).

§7. Works of Public Undertaking

84. Where a public undertaking is the first owner of the copyright in a work, copyright will subsist for sixty years from the year in which it is first published. A public undertaking means:

(1) a Government undertaking;
(2) a Government Company as defined in section 2(45) of Companies Act, 2013; or
(3) a body corporate established by any Government[84] (section 28(A)).

§8. Work of International Organizations

85. Copyright subsists until sixty years from the calendar year following the year in which the work is first published (section 29).

§9. Broadcast Reproduction Rights

86. These rights subsist until twenty-five years from the beginning of the calendar year following the year in which the broadcast is made. Although the broadcast reproduction rights will expire twenty-five years from the year following the broadcast, the copyright in the script and music will continue to subsist until the term of copyright appropriate to them expires (section 37(2)).

83. Miss Kajal Aggarwal v. The Managing Director, M/s V.V. D & Sons Pvt. Ltd OS App.
84. See s. 17(dd), inserted by Copyright (Amendment) Act, 1983.

§10. Performing Rights

87. The performing rights will subsist until fifty years from the beginning of the calendar year following the year in which the performance is made (section 38(2)).

Chapter 9. Performing Rights

88. Section 38 of the Act deals with performers' rights. The lack of some kind of right to the performance of an actor, musician and dancer and so on was a major disadvantage in copyright law. This section introduces the concept of moral rights of the performers in the integrity of their performance. The Copyright (Amendment) Act of 1994, for the first time, introduced special rights called performers' rights for the benefit of various kinds of performers like actors, dancers, musicians, jugglers, acrobats, etc. This was further extensively amended by the Copyright (Amendment) Act, 2012. Where any performer appears or engages in any performance, he/she shall have a special right to be known as the 'performer's right' in relation to such performance.[85] These rights are more or less analogous to broadcast reproduction rights.[86]

89. The term 'performer', according to section 2(qq), includes an acrobat, musician, singer, actor, juggler, snake charmer, a person delivering a lecture or any other person who makes a performance. As per section 2(q), 'performance', in relation to performers' rights, means any visual or acoustic presentation made live by one or more performers. A cricket match has been held to be a 'performance' within the meaning of the Act.[87] A further specification comes by way of the Copyright Rules, 2013, that performance includes recording of visual or acoustic presentation of a performer in the studio or otherwise.[88] The performers' rights will subsist for fifty years from the beginning of the year following the year of performance. When a performance is incorporated in a cinematograph film, through a written agreement, the performer shall not object to the producer enjoying the performer's right in the same film if there is no contract to that effect. However, the performer shall be entitled to royalties in case the performance is exploited for commercial use.[89] The term 'commercial use' is defined in Explanation 2 of Rule 68, the Copyright Rules, 2013, as *the exploitation of the performer's right by way of reproduction, issue of copies or distribution, communicating to public, including broadcasting and commercial rental of the cinematograph film*. The royalty collected from enjoyment of the performer's right is to be shared equally between the performer and the other owner of the copyright.[90] This was specifically introduced by the Copyright (Amendment) Act, 2012, in order to protect the performers' right to receive royalties for the commercial exploitation of his/her work, except when the performance is incorporated in a cinematograph film.

The jurisprudence has been developed on this issue by the Supreme Court in the case of *CISAC v. Aditya Pandey*.[91] The issue of contention was what happens to the copyright in an underlying work (literary and musical works) when the derivative

85. Section 38(1).
86. Section 39A.
87. Star India Pvt. Ltd. v. Piyush Agarwal & Ors. (2014) 58 PTC 169 (Del).
88. Explanation 3 of Rule 68, The Copyright Rules, 2013.
89. Section 38A.
90. Explanation 1 of Rule 68, The Copyright Rules, 2013.
91. International Confederation of Societies of Authors and Composers (CISAC) v. Aditya Pandey C A Nos 9412–9413 OF 2016.

work (sound recording) is exploited. Is there a need for an individual who wishes to use said derivative work to secure permission from both the owner of the derivative work and the owners of the underlying work, that is, the lyricists and composer? The Supreme Court provided a partial relief by holding that lyricists and composers shall be entitled to royalty only in a scenario where the sound recording does not form part of any cinematographic film.

The performer has the exclusive right to do the following:

- to make sound recording or visual recording of the performance, including:
  (1) reproduction of it in any material form, including the storing of it in any medium by electronic or any other means;
  (2) issuance of copies in public not being copies in circulation;
  (3) communication in public; and
  (4) selling or giving it on commercial rental or offer for sale or for commercial rental any copy of the recording.
- to broadcast or communicate the performance to the public, except where the performance is already broadcast.

Section 38B provides moral rights to the performers, similar to section 57. Two moral rights have been specified:

- to claim to be identified as the performer of his performance, except where omission is dictated by the manner of the use of the performance; and
- to restrain or claim damages in respect of any distortion, mutilation or other modification of his/her performance that would be prejudicial to his/her reputation.

Section 38B further clarifies that a mere removal of any portion of a performance for the purpose of editing, or to fit the recording within a limited duration, or any other modification required for purely technical reasons, shall not be deemed to be prejudicial to the performer's reputation.

90. According to section 39, the following acts do not constitute infringement of a performer's right in his/her performance:

- the making of any sound recording of or visual recording for private use of the person making such recording or solely for the purpose of bona fide teaching or research; or
- the use, consistent with fair dealing, of excerpts of a performance in the reporting of current events or for bona fide review, teaching or research; or
- such other acts, with any necessary adaptations and modifications, which do not constitute infringement of copyright under section 52.

91. Where copyright or performer's right subsists in respect of any work or performance that has been broadcast, a licence to reproduce such broadcast will require the consent of the owner of the right or the performer, as the case may be, or both of them. But the broadcast reproduction right or performer's right shall not subsist in any broadcast or performance if that broadcast or performance is an infringement of the copyright in any work.[92]

92. Section 39A(1).

Chapter 10. Infringement and Remedies

§1. Direct Infringement of Copyright in Works

92. As per section 51, copyright in a work is deemed to be infringed when any person, without a licence from the owner of the copyright, or the Registrar of Copyright, or in contravention of the conditions of a licence granted or any conditions imposed by a competent authority under the Act:

- does anything, the exclusive right to do which is conferred upon the owner of the copyright; or
- permits, for profit, any place to be used for the communication of the work to the public, where such communication constitutes an infringement of the copyright in the work, unless he/she was not aware and had no reasonable ground for believing that such communication to the public would be an infringement of copyright; or
- makes for sale or hire, or sells or lets for hire or by way of trade displays or offers for sale or hire any infringing copies of the work; or
- distributes, either for the purpose of trade or to such an extent as to affect prejudicially the owner of the copyright, any infringing copies of the work; or
- exhibits in public by way of trade any infringing copies of the work; or
- imports into India any infringing copies of the work, except one copy of any work for the private and domestic use of the importer.

The reproduction of a literary, dramatic, musical or artistic work in the form of a cinematograph film will be deemed to be an infringing copy. The definition of the term 'infringing copy', as stated in section 2(m) of the Act, includes a reproduction of a literary, dramatic, musical or artistic work, a copy of a film, a sound recording or a cinematographic film or a sound recording of a programme or performance, made or imported in contravention of the Act. Therefore, in the case of literary, dramatic, musical or artistic work in which copyright subsists, to make any adaptation of the work without the consent of the owner of the copyright amounts to infringement.[93] Publishing the work of an author in another person's name, without the consent of the author, will also constitute an infringement of copyright.[94] However, if an author permits his/her book to be published by a university as part of its syllabus, the book goes into the public domain, and no copyright remains with the author.[95]

93. The onus of proving infringement of copyright is on the plaintiff. Whether the work complained of is or is not a colourable imitation of another is a question

93. Section 14. See also Barbara Taylor Bradford v. Sahara Media Entertainment Ltd (2003) 47 SCL 445 Cal.
94. Thankappan v. Vidyarambham Press (1968) Ker LJ 440. Federation of Industries & Another v. G. Kesavulu Naidu (2011) 48 PTC 496 (Del).
95. Ramesh Chowdhury and Ors v. Kh. Ali Mohammad AIR 1965 J&K 101.

of fact, and the burden of proving that fact is on the plaintiff.[96] In order to constitute infringement, there should be direct or indirect use of those features of the plaintiff's works in which copyright subsists.[97] It is difficult to be precise as to the amount of copying or degree of resemblance necessary to constitute infringement. It really depends on the effect produced on the mind by a study of work and of that which is alleged to be a copy of it.[98] It is not an essential ingredient of infringement that the transgressor had an intention to infringe.[99] As long as there is some form of copying, direct, indirect or even subconscious, it will amount to infringement. Whether or not there has been a violation of copyright is to see if the reader, spectator or the viewer after having read or seen both the works is clearly of the opinion and gets an unmistakable impression that the subsequent work appears to be a copy of the original.[100] Since copyright is not vested in an idea, and only the original expression of an idea is protected, the enquiry of originality of the work from the author is the basic test for an infringement claim.[101]

94. If any person, without a licence from the copyright owner, imports a literary work into India for the purposes of sale, distribution or trade, copyright is infringed even if the work was lawfully published by the owner of the copyright or the exclusive licensee in the country from which it has been imported. This is clear from the definition of infringing copy in section 2(m) read with sections 51 and 53(1). The importer of a copyright work, lawfully purchased in one country, would be subject to the laws of the particular country to which it is imported.[102] The word 'import' has been interpreted to mean 'bringing into India from outside India' and includes not only importation for commerce but also importation for transit across India.[103] An interesting variation has been in the case of cybercrimes, where cybersquatting has been brought within the jurisdiction of Indian courts on the ground that the internet is available in India and thus, potentially, a cause of action can be made out in relation to anything available via the internet. To combat situations like these, courts often pass John Doe orders against the unnamed defendants to prevent them from hosting and selling pirated content on their websites.

95. On the question of violation of copyright owner's rights, an interesting legal case and debate is carrying on in India. The case concerns two entities, namely Scihub and Library Genesis (LibGen), which are websites that provide access to scholarly books, articles, research papers and magazines, and since the content that they host is

96. Mishra Bandhu Karvalaya and Ors v. Shivratanlal Koshan AIR 1976 MP 26.
97. Divya Sood Proprietor M/s The Body Care v. Renu Bajaj Proprietor M/S. Perfect Body Care (2011) 45 PTC 307 (Del).
98. K.S. Gita v. Vision Time Pvt. Ltd. And Others (2011) 45 PTC 393 (Mad).
99. Lahari Recording Company Limited v. Music Master Video Manufacturing Co. Ltd. (2008) 37 PTC 121 (Mad).
100. C. Cunniah & Co. v. Balraj & Co., AIR 1961 Mad 111, K. R. Venugopala Sarma v. Sangu Ganesan (1972) Cri.LJ 1098 (Mad); Associated Electronic and Electric Industries, Bangalore Pvt Ltd v. Sharp Tools AIR 1991 Kar 406; Barbara Taylor Bradford v. Sahara Media Entertainment Ltd (2003) 47 SCL 445 Cal.
101. Institute for Inner Studies & Ors. v. Charlotte Anderson & Ors. (2014) 57 PTC 228 (Del).
102. Penguin Books v. India Book AIR 1985 Del 29 at 33 (DB).
103. Gramophone Company of India Ltd. v. Birendra Bahadur Pandey, and Others AIR (1984) SC 667.

often under copyright protection, a few publishers have approached the Delhi High Court to seek a dynamic injunction and block access to them forever in India.[104]

96. The case is fascinating because it brings into focus the competing claims of the publisher's rights versus the benefits accrued to many researchers and students who cannot access pay-walled content through these websites. Given the nature of this matter and the far-reaching implications of it, the Delhi High Court is presently taking submissions of any intervening parties in this matter.

§2. Indirect Infringement of Copyright in Works

97. Indirect copying is considered infringement so long as the tests provided above are met.

§3. Remedies: Civil

98. The civil remedies available to a plaintiff include injunction, damages and accounts, delivery of infringing copies and damages for conversion under section 55.

99. Injunction: Injunction is the most important remedy against infringement. The High Courts of India have been active in granting protection against infringement in the form of interlocutory injunction. As litigation can be time-consuming, often adequate relief is provided by this alone. The following types of injunction may be granted:

– Interlocutory injunction.[105]
– Mandatory injunction.[106]
– Permanent injunction.[107]

Within the ambit of interlocutory injunctions, the courts provide for John Doe orders in scenarios where the defendant is an unnamed entity. These injunctions are largely used in cases to prevent the defendants from hosting pirated content. This is done by enabling the plaintiffs to restrict websites and ISPs from hosting pirated films and other such content.

However, a series of orders passed by the Bombay High Court[108] laid down a strict framework for grant of John Doe orders. These guidelines aim at balancing

104. Elsevier Ltd. & Ors. v. Alexandra Elbakyan & Ors. CS(COMM) No. 572 of 2020.
105. R.M. Subbiah and Another v. N. Sankaran Nair and Another, AIR 1979 Mad 56.
106. Channuapati v. Boooboala AIR 1977 NOC 257 (AP).
107. Mirabai Films Pvt. Limited & Ors. v. Hathway Cable and Datacom Pvt. Ltd. (2002) 25 PTC 148 (Del).
108. Rahul Bajaj, Bombay HC Effectively Transforms John Does from Swords to Shields – Delineates Most Robust Safeguards to Date, SPICY IP (28 Jul. 2016) https://spicyip.com/2016/07/bombay-hc-effectively-transforms-john-does-from-swords-to-shields-delineates-most-robust-safeguards-to-date.html.

the interests of the copyright holders as well as that of the internet users and innocent third-party providers. The court reiterated that only the specific infringing links can be blocked and not the entire website. For any such blocking orders to be issued, the links need to be verified by a technically competent person and listed on the affidavit that a specific blocking message must be displayed by the ISPs and that third parties injured by John Doe order can approach the court for relief.

Furthermore, orders such as the Anton Pillar Order[109] prevent the defendant from dealing in the infringing goods or destroying them, along with the fact that they allow for the defendant's premises to be searched to secure said goods. Orders such as the Mareva Injunctions temporarily freeze the assets of a defendant, thus preventing him/her from frustrating the judgment by disposal of such assets.[110] The power is by Order 49 of the Criminal Procedure Code, though the principles are similar to Order 48. Lastly, the Norwich Pharmaceutical Orders[111] provide for the cooperation from third parties involved in the infringing/unlawful activity to provide information to the individual suffering damage due to the defendant's unlawful conduct by disclosing their identities.

100. Damages: There are two types of damages available to the owner of a copyright, one under section 55, for infringement, and the other under section 58, for conversion. Copyright infringement is a tort, thereby requiring compensatory damages.[112] A plaintiff may claim both damages for infringement and those for conversion, as they are cumulative and not mutually exclusive.[113] Although these two remedies are not alternative but cumulative, in some cases where the plaintiff obtains damages for infringement, he/she may not be able to recover any damages for conversion.[114] Damages are awarded only in rare instances by Indian Courts.[115]

101. Account of profits: It means that the defendant is required to account for the profits made by him by infringing the plaintiff's copyright.[116] A plaintiff cannot claim both damages and account of profits.[117] Only one out of the two remedies can be claimed.

102. Conversion: As per the provisions of section 58, all infringing copies of any work in which copyright subsists, as well as all plates used or intended to be used for the production of such infringing copies, are deemed to be the property of the

109. Derives its name from the Court of Appeal decision in Anton Pillar AG v. Manufacturing Processes [1976] Ch. 55.
110. Derives its name from the case of Mareva Compania Naviera SA v. International Bulkcarriers SA The Mareva [1980] 1 All ER 213.
111. Derives its name from the case of Norwich Pharmacal Co. & Others v. Customs and Excise Commissioners [1974] AC 133.
112. Microsoft Corporation v. K. Mayuri & Ors. (2007) 35 PTC 415 (Del); Indian Performing Rights Society Ltd. v. Debashis Patnaik & Ors (2007) 34 PTC 415 (Del).
113. Caxton Publishing Co v. Sutherland Publishing (1938) 4 All ER 389 (HL).
114. S.B. Yeates v. Eric Dickinson AIR 1938 Lah 273.
115. Hawkins Cookers Ltd. v. Magicook Appliances Co. (2002) 25 PTC 713 (Del); Diamond Comic Pvt. Ltd. And Anr. v. Raja Pocket Books and Others (2005) 31 PTC 378 (Del).
116. Super Cassettes Industries Ltd. v. Onkar Singh & Ors. (2014) 57 PTC 460 (Del).
117. Pillalamari Lakshmikanthan v. Ramakrishna Pictures AIR 1981 AP 224.

owner of the copyright. He/she has the right to recover possession of the infringing copies that have not yet been sold and the price of copies that have been sold. The only exception is where the defendant proves that he/she was not aware and had no reasonable grounds to believe that copyright subsists in the work or that he/she had reasonable grounds to believe that such copies or plates do not involve infringement of the copyright in any work.

103. Discovery and Inspection: The rules governing discovery and inspection contained in Order 11 of the Code of Civil Procedure apply to copyright cases also.

104. Discovery of defendants' customers: The court has jurisdiction to order the disclosure of names and addresses of defendants' customers.[118]

105. Discovery of the names of wrongdoers: The court has jurisdiction to order discovery of the names of wrongdoers.

§4. Criminal Offences and Penalties

106. Offences: Conduct of criminal proceedings under the Act is governed by the provisions of the Criminal Procedure Code. The following are criminal offences under the Act:

- Section 63: Offence of knowingly committing infringement or abetment of such infringement of copyright in a work, or any other right conferred by this Act, except the right conferred by section 53(A), which is the right to share in the resale price of the original work.
- Section 63(B): Knowing the use of an infringing copy of a computer program.
- Section 65: Possession of plates for the purpose of making infringing copies.
- Section 65A: Any person who circumvents an effective technological measure applied for the purpose of protecting any of the rights conferred by this Act, with the intention of infringing such rights, shall be punishable with imprisonment, which may extend to two years and a fine. But section 65B does not prohibit any act for the purpose of conducting encryption research, lawful investigation or taking measures in the interest of national security.[119]
- Section 67: Making false entries in the Register of Copyrights kept under this Act.
- Section 68: Making false statements for the purpose of deceiving or influencing any authority or officer under the Act.
- Section 68(A): Contravention of section 52(A) regarding particulars to be included in sound recordings and video films.

107. Penalties: The penalties provided for criminal offences under the Act include imprisonment of the accused, imposition of a fine, both imprisonment and

118. Ibid., at 88.
119. Section 65A(2).

a fine, seizure of infringing copies and delivery of infringing copies to the owner of the copyright.[120] Knowledge, or mens rea, is an essential ingredient of the offence.[121] Civil remedies and criminal proceedings against the infringer are distinct and independent and can be availed of simultaneously. The court has the discretion to reduce the minimum term of imprisonment and the minimum fine for adequate and special reasons where the infringement has not been made for gain in the course of trade or business. What are adequate and special reasons will be for the court to determine, having regard to the particular circumstances of the trade.

120. Sections 63 and 64.
121. Sections 63, 65B.

Chapter 11. Relation to Other Intellectual Property Rights

108. Registered designs under the Designs Act, 2000, are not entitled to protection under the Copyright Act. Any design not registered under the Designs Act, 2000, or its predecessor, the Designs Act of 1911, will be eligible for protection under the Copyright Act. Any design capable of being registered as a design shall be eligible for protection under section 15 of the Copyright Act. This protection shall cease as soon as the design has been produced more than fifty times by an industrial process by the owner of the copyright or his/her licensee.[122] Another area of overlap is with respect to broadcast rights, which are for twenty-five years. Copyright, such as the script and music and performers' rights, runs concurrently and may survive the broadcast rights for the full term of sixty years, as the case may be.

122. Microlube India Limited v. Rakesh Kumar (2013) 55 PTC 61 (Del); Jagdamba Impex v. Tristar Products Private Ltd. (2014) 59 PTC 149 (Del); Urooj Ahmed v. Preethi Kitchen Appliances P. Ltd. (2014) 57 PTC 139 (Del).

Part II. Patents

Chapter 1. Sources – Legislation

109. The first statute relating to patent rights in India was passed in 1856, which granted certain exclusive privileges to inventors for a period of fourteen years. This Act was re-enacted with modifications in 1859. The provisions of this Act were based on the English Patent Act of 1852. The Protection of Invention Act was passed in 1888. However, when the Indian Patents & Designs Act of 1911 was enacted, it replaced all previous legislations on the subject of patent rights. In the period between 1911 and 1970, various amendments to the Act of 1911 were made from time to time. The legislation that governs patent law in India is the Patents Act, 1970 (The Act), as amended by the Patents (Amendment) Act, 1999, the Patents (Amendment) Act, 2002, and the Patents (Amendment) Act, 2005, and the Rules made thereunder. The Patents Act of 1970 sought to balance protection of patents with the developmental, technological and public interest needs of India. It did not allow product patents for pharmaceuticals and agrochemicals. The focus was on protecting public interest and building up domestic technological capability. The pharmaceutical industry in particular benefited, and India has some of the lowest prices for pharmaceuticals in the world. The Constitution of India 1950, by including patents as an item in the Union List, has mandated that all powers to legislate on the subject shall vest with the Parliament.

110. While TRIPS became an agreement under the World Trade Organization (WTO), there is a countervailing movement among developing countries and public interest groups involved in health-related issues worldwide to prevent unnecessary barriers in access to medicine, which will lead to an increase in mortality from preventable illness. These groups seek to exempt all drugs on the essential drugs list of the World Health Organization (WHO) from patentability. The last substantial amendments were made in 2005 in the law. These amendments were remarkable, for they sought to keep medicines at an affordable rate by ensuring that India developed strong standards (in consonance with WTO norms) for patents in a bid to promote genuine innovation across all realms of technology. In spite of protests by generic drug manufacturers and various Non-governmental Organizations (NGOs), the Government has maintained that India cannot renege on its international obligations. Over fifteen official amendments were included to accommodate the points raised by the Left Parties.

111. In 2001, India developed a system of tabulating resources on traditional knowledge similar to the International Patent Classification (IPC). The IPC is expected to include about two hundred drugs derived from medicinal plants in their own Classification. The Government is also creating an Atlas of bio-resources to help protect items from being patented by foreign companies.

Chapter 2. Patentable Subject Matter

112. A patent is granted to an invention, not a discovery. The invented substance itself or the process leading up to that invention may be patented. Section 2(1)(j) of the Patents Act, 1970, defines an invention as any new product or process involving an inventive step capable of industrial application. After the 2005 Amendments, two new definitions were added, i.e., inventive step and new invention. Under section 2(1)(j) of the Act, 'inventive step' means a feature of an invention that involves technical advance, as compared to the existing knowledge or having economic significance or both, that makes that invention not obvious to a person skilled in the art. Section 2(1)(l) defines 'new invention' as any invention or technology which has not been anticipated by publication in any document or used in the country or elsewhere in the world before the date of filing of patent application.

113. Section 3 of the Act lists several items that cannot be patented, like inventions that are frivolous, or are contrary to law or morality, or are mere admixtures, arrangement or rearrangement of known devices, or are methods of agriculture or horticulture, or any process for the medicinal, surgical, prophylactic or other treatment of human beings, plants and animals among others. Under the Patents (Amendment) Act, 2005, a computer program per se has been made unpatentable.[123] An exception is made for a computer program's technical application to industry and a combination of software and hardware. However, in June 2013, the Indian Patent Office released draft guidelines for the examination of Computer-Related Invention (CRI) to invite public comments. The guidelines provide standards/procedures to determine whether the CRI claims fall under the scope of non-patentable subject matter under section 3k of the India Patent Act, 1970 (as amended). While feedback has been provided by various stakeholders to draft the guidelines, the patent office has changed its stance on numerous occasions in the intervening. As of July 2017, based on the submissions, the patent office released a new set of guidelines which provide for a new two-step test to determine the applicability of section 3(k):[124]

(1) Properly construe the claim and identify the actual contribution.
(2) If the contribution lies only in mathematical method, business method or algorithm, deny the claim.

114. Previously, there existed a requirement of patents on software being sought in conjunction with the hardware, but that was scrapped by the 2017 guidelines. This move would make securing a patent on a software a far easier task than before.

115. Section 3(d) provides that the mere discovery of a new form of a known substance, which does not result in the enhancement of the known efficacy of that

123. Section 3(k), The Patents Act, 1970.
124. Revised Guidelines for Examination of Computer-Related Inventions (CRIs) published. 'Guidelines' l 'Office Order' – http://www.ipindia.nic.in/newsdetail.htm?351. These guidelines were originally introduced in 2016 as three-point guidelines with modification being made to it in 2017.

substance, does not constitute 'invention'. Further, section 3(d) provides that the mere discovery of any new property or new use of a known process, machine, or apparatus, unless such known process results in a new product or employs at least one new reactant, does not amount to 'invention'. Section 4 similarly prohibits the granting of any patent to an invention relating to atomic energy. Furthermore, section 5 under the 1999 amendment restricted the grant of product patents to inventions relating to drugs, food or medicines but allowed methods or processes of manufacture to be patented. However, this section has been omitted from the principal Act, under the Patents (Amendment) Act, 2005, and after 2005, product patents for pharmaceutical products are now recognized in India.

There has been considerable controversy in India over the patenting of Indian food products in the USA. Section 3(p) states that an invention which, in effect, is traditional knowledge or which is an aggregation or duplication of known properties of a traditionally known component or components cannot be patented. The Government of India has taken steps to challenge the grant of patents which do not conform to the standards of patentability in India.[125] India's effort has been to protect the knowledge of indigenous communities from commercialization by multinational corporations. There have been numerous instances of multinational corporations seeking IPR protection for traditional Indian plants and medicinal herbs. Some notable instances from the last decade are as follows:

- On 21 May 2003, Monsanto Technology was granted a patent for Nap Hal, a traditional Indian wheat variety crossed with another wheat line. The NGO Greenpeace India has decided to file an objection to the patent in the European Patent Office, which was finally revoked in October 2014.
- India won a decade-long battle against the granting of a patent to a neem-based crop fungicide by the European Patent Office (EPO) by proving that it was part of the traditional knowledge of Indian farmers.
- Multinational corporations have claimed rights over Haldi (a commonly used spice with anti-inflammatory properties) and Basmati Rice, which were both revoked later on.
- Indian Yoga guru Bikram Chaudhary obtained patents, copyrights and trademarks over various yoga asanas in the US, which were opposed by the Indian Government and were later revoked by the US patent office.
- The US consumer giant Colgate-Palmolive tried to claim patents over two oral compositions of toothpaste made from traditional Indian herbs and spices, but these claims were rejected by the EPO in June 2015, based on India's traditional knowledge digital library database.

Similarly, there have been lots of debates regarding the patenting of microorganisms in India. Though earlier microorganisms were not subject to product patents, India started granting patents on microorganisms from 20 May 2003 onwards. Currently, there are restrictions on the patenting of microorganisms:

125. Research Foundation for Science Technology & Ecology v. Ministry of Agriculture (1999) 1 SCC 655.

- Section 3(b) excludes an invention whose primary use or commercial exploitation causes serious prejudice to humans, animals or plants.
- Section 3(c) prohibits patents on naturally occurring microorganisms.
- Section 3(j) bars patents on plants and animals, in whole or in part, except microorganisms, but including seeds, varieties and species.

Reading all these together, it is evident that genetically modified versions of the same microorganisms that result in the enhancement of their known efficacies are patentable.[126] The procedure to apply for patent for microorganisms with complete specification is mentioned in section 10(d) proviso (ii).

116. An invention may be said to be patentable where the component elements are so combined as to produce a new result or to arrive at an old result in a better or more expeditious or more economical manner. So, if a product is substantially improved by an inventive step, it would be called an invention.[127] However, the mere bringing together of two or more things, without any exercise of the inventive faculty in combining them, is not subject matter for a patent. The inventor, in the case of a combination, may act on a number of principles that are well known, but if he/she experimented in order to see which combination produced a new and useful result and if he/she succeeds in ascertaining that such a result is arrived at by a particular combination, the combination will be the subject matter for a patent.[128] Thus, a mere juxtaposition of features already known before the priority date, which have arbitrarily been chosen from among a number of different combinations that could be chosen, was not a patentable invention. Further, when two or more features of an apparatus or device are known and they are juxtaposed without any interdependence on the functioning of the apparatus or device, it should be held to have been already known and therefore not patentable (*Ram Pratap v. Bhabha Atomic Research Centre* (1976) IPLR 28).

If the invention is obvious, then there exists no inventive step.[129] With the new definition of 'inventive step' from 2005 onwards, Courts have interpreted inventive step accordingly.[130]

117. The definition of an invention includes any new and useful improvement of any manner of manufacture, article or substance, whether patented or otherwise. However, the improvement itself, in order to be patentable, must independently satisfy the test of invention. An invention to be patentable must relate to a new and useful method of manufacture of some product or article. The term 'manner of manufacture' has been interpreted to include not only a process of manufacture but

---

126. Shradha Diwan, Patentability of Microorganisms, INSTITUTE OF INTERNATIONAL TRADE (5 Feb. 2008), http://iitrade.ac.in/kmarticle.php?topic=Patentability%20of%20Microorganisms.
127. Dhanpath Seth & Ors. v. Nil Kamal Plastic Crates Ltd. (2008) 36 PTC 123 (HP).
128. Lallubhai Chakubhai Jariwala v. Chimanlal Chunilal & Co, AIR 1936 Bom 99.
129. Press Metal Corporation Limited v. Noshir Sorabji Pochkhanwalla & Anr. AIR 1983 Bom 144.
130. Bajaj Auto Ltd. v. TVS Motor Company (2008) 36 PTC 417 (Mad); F. Hoffman-La-Roche Ltd. & Anr. v. Cipla Limited (2008) 37 PTC 71 (Del); Mariappan v. A.R. Safiullah & Ors. (2008) 38 PTC 341 (Mad).

also a manufactured product. If the starting material remains unaltered by the process and the end product is the same as the starting material, then the process cannot be called a 'manner of manufacture' for the purpose of patentability. An art, process or method to be patentable must result in the production of something, such as a machine, an apparatus, an article or a substance. A method of generating electricity cannot be considered to be a 'manner of manufacture', under section 2(1)(j) read with Rule 2(c) of the rules.[131] It has also been held that a new and alternative method of arriving at the same result, irrespective of whether the result is better or cheaper, may be patentable.[132]

118. The word 'manufacture' has been generally understood to either denote a thing made, which is useful for its own sake, and vendible as such, as a medicine, a stove, a telescope, and many others, or to mean an engine or instrument to be employed either in the making of some previously known article or in some other useful purpose, as a stocking-frame, or a steam engine for raising water from mines, or it may perhaps extend also to a new process to be carried on by known implements, or elements, acting upon known substances, and ultimately producing some other known substance, but producing it in a cheaper or more expeditious manner, or of a better or more useful kind. But no merely philosophical or abstract principle can answer to the word 'manufacture'. Something of a corporal and substantial nature, something that can be made by man from the matters subjected to his/her art and skill, or at the least some new mode of employing practically his/her art and skill, is requisite to satisfy this word.[133]

119. Judicial interpretation of the term 'manner of manufacture' has endowed it with a special signification in relation to patent law. In G.E.C.'s Appln.,[134] J. Morton referring to the line to be drawn between a method or process which is a manner of manufacture and a method or process which is not a manner of manufacture, stated:

> A method or process is a manner of manufacture if it:
>
> (a) results in the production of some vendible product;
> (b) improves or restores to its former condition a vendible product; or
> (c) has the effect of preserving from deterioration some vendible product to which it is applied.

120. In order to decide whether a particular invention sought to be patented is a 'manner of manufacture' as per the meaning of the definition in the Patents Act,

131. Snamprogetti S.P.A.'s Appln. 2 DPD 60.
132. It has been observed by the Controller General that generally a process is considered to be new if: (a) it results in a new product; (b) it uses new starting materials; or (c) it employs a novel combination of steps even if such steps themselves may not be per se novel, Catalysts & Chemicals India (West Asia) Ltd v. Imperial Chemical Industries Ltd (1976) IPLR 84.
133. R v. Wheeler (1819) 2 B. & ald 345; quoted and followed in Bombay Agarwal Co. v. Ramchand, AIR 1953 Nagpur 154.
134. (1943) 60 R.P.C. 1.

1970, certain tests as laid down by courts have to be applied. However, the concept of vendibility of a product has not been adopted by the Patent Office in India while considering whether a method or process is a manner of manufacture. Courts have held that a process of manufacture is independent of the substance produced by the manufacture and has a distinctive identity of its own unconnected with the final product.[135] Where a process patent was obtained after prolonged research work, it was held that it would be possible to predict that the substance was produced by that process.[136]

After 2005, product patents for pharmaceuticals began to be granted.

135. Thomson Brandt v. Controller of Patents, AIR 1989 Del 249.
136. Farbewerke Hoechst Aktiengesellschaft Vormals Meister Lucius & Brunning Corporation v. Unichem Laboratories, AIR 1969 Bom 255.

Chapter 3. Conditions of Patentability

121. A patent is granted only to an invention that is new and useful. The three conditions that are therefore required to be present in an invention for it to be patentable are:

(1) novelty;
(2) utility; and
(3) inventive step.

122. Novelty: 'Novelty' means that which is new and original and has not been seen or done before. As per the definition of 'invention' given in the Act of 1970, novelty in the invention is an essential prerequisite for obtaining a patent. However, the determination of whether an invention involves novelty is both a question of law and fact and depends on the circumstances of each case.[137] The Supreme Court has held that *'the fundamental principle of patent law is that a patent is granted only for invention, which must be new and useful. That is to say, it must have novelty and utility. It is essential for the validity of a patent that it must be the inventor's own discovery as opposed to mere verification of what was already known before the date of the patent'*.[138] What is certain is that a patentee must use his/her knowledge and ingenuity so as to produce either a new and useful thing or result or a new method of producing an old thing or result.[139] The description of the invention must be found to be novel, prima facie, before the full description of the invention is assessed, and the invention must involve an inventive step having novelty and utility.[140] Thus, a new product in chemicals and especially pharmaceuticals may not necessarily mean something altogether new or completely unfamiliar or strange or not existing before. It may mean something different from a recent previous.[141]

123. An invention may be held invalid if the matter contained therein was:

(1) publicly known or publicly used in India before the priority date of the claim under section 25 of Patents Act, 1970; or
(2) published in India or elsewhere in any specification filed in connection with an application for a patent made after 1 January 1912 or in any other document. Thus, in the case of patents granted under the previous Act, documents published outside India will not be taken into consideration for determining whether the claim is anticipated by prior publication. But under the present law, for the purpose of determining novelty, documents published anywhere in the world will be considered with this act of determination being called as prior art as encapsulated under section 29 of the Patents Act, 1970.

---

137. Bishwanath Prasad Radhey Shyam v. Hindustan Metal Industries (1979) 2 SCC 511 at 519.
138. Ibid., at p. 517.
139. Lane-Fox v. Kensington, RPC 413 at 416, Lallubhai Chakubhai Jariwala v. Samaldas Shah AIR 1934 Bom 407.
140. Bishwanath Prasad Radhey Shyam v. Hindustan Metal Industries (1979) 2 SCC 511.
141. Novartis AG v. Union of India & Ors. (2013) 6 SCC 1.

124. The procedure laid down under section 13 states that the examiner has to ascertain whether any claim made in the complete specification accompanying a patent application is anticipated by prior publication of the matter either in a patent specification or in any other document published in India or elsewhere.[142] It further states that this examination shall not be deemed in any way to warrant the validity of any patent, and no liability shall be incurred by the Central Government or any officer thereof.[143] Thus, the grant of patent does not guarantee the validity of the patent.[144] Section 14 provides that if the patent examiner's report is adverse to the applicant or requires an amendment in the application/specification, the Controller shall communicate the said objections to the applicant and provide him/her an opportunity of being heard, before deciding the application. The courts have held that this is a substantive provision requiring consideration of the report of the examiner by the Patent Controller.[145] Section 15 mandates that if the Controller is satisfied that application/specification/documents filed by the applicant do not comply with the requirements of the Act, then he/she can refuse the application.[146] Section 64(1)(e) and (f) provides that a patent may be revoked on, *inter alia*, the ground of lack of novelty or obviousness. It also details the facts to be taken into consideration in determining lack of novelty or anticipation. Circumstances where prior publication or prior use does not constitute anticipation are given in sections 29–34. In fact, the Controller shall not refuse to grant a patent or revoke/invalidate a patent if any of the circumstances under sections 29/30/31/32 do not constitute anticipation of the invention claimed in the specification.[147]

125. Utility*:* The second essential requirement of a patentable invention is that it should be useful. It follows that a patent, which is not useful, is capable of being revoked on the ground of non-utility. The meaning of the term 'useful' in patent law is different from the meaning of the term as used in commercial parlance. It basically means that the invention is capable of industrial application; i.e., the invention is capable of being made or used in an industry.[148]

126. Whether an invention is useful in patent law is tested by determining if the invention works/operates at all, or more broadly, that it does what the specification promises that it will do. The practical usefulness or commercial utility of the invention is of no consequence, and it does not matter whether the invention is of any real benefit to the public or if it is particularly suitable for the purposes suggested. That is, mere usefulness is not sufficient to warrant a patent.[149] Although, generally, commercial success has no relation to the question of utility in patent law, where

142. Rules 28 and 30, Patents Rules, 2003.
143. Section 13(4).
144. M/s Standipack Pvt. Ltd. v. Oswal Trading Co. Ltd. & Others AIR 2000 Del 23; J. Mitra and Co. Ltd. v. Kesar Medicaments (2008) 36 PTC 568 (Del); Bajaj Auto Ltd. v. TVS Motor Co. Ltd. (2008) 36 PTC 417.
145. Ferid Allani v. Union of India (2008) 37 PTC 448 (Del).c
146. Yahoo! Inc v. Intellectual Property Appellate Board (2010) 44 PTC 8 (Mad).
147. Section 34, The Patents Act, 1970.
148. Section 2(1)(ac).
149. Indian Vacuum Brake Co. Ltd. v. E.S. Luard, AIR 1926 Cal 152.

the question is of improvement by reason of cheaper production, such a consideration is of the very essence of the patent itself, and the thing claimed cannot be considered an invention unless that condition is fulfilled.[150]

127. The utility of the patent must be judged by reference to the state of things at the date of the patent; if the invention was useful at that point of time, the fact that subsequent improvements have replaced the patented invention and rendered it obsolete and commercially of no value does not invalidate the patent.[151]

128. It is also not necessary that a new result should be obtained by using the invention and that the test is whether the new method gives the public a useful choice.[152] Only failure of the invention to produce the results that have been promised will invalidate the patent.[153]

129. Inventive step: A patentable invention must involve the exercise of inventive powers or the innovative faculty. The mere discovery of a scientific principle or the formulation of an abstract theory is not an invention as per the Act.[154] An invention, to be patentable, has to be non-obvious. Obviousness and inventiveness are antitheses. What is obvious cannot be inventive, and what is inventive cannot be obvious.[155] The word 'obvious' is used in its normal sense of something which is plain or open to the eye or mind, something which is perfectly evident to a person thinking on the subject.[156] In other words, the invention must be obvious to a skilled technician who is well acquainted with the relevant techniques and who has carefully read the relevant literature. However, the question to be asked is not whether it was obvious to the inventor or to some other particular worker in the field.[157]

The *U.S. Supreme Court in Graham v. John Deere Co.*[158] laid down certain criteria to determine obviousness, namely: (i) the scope and content of prior art, (ii) the difference between prior art and the claims at issue, (iii) the level of ordinary skill in the pertinent art.[159]

---

150. Badische Anilin und Soda Fabric v. Levinstein, 4 RPC 449 at 462 (HL), per Lord Chancellor.
151. Edison and Swan Electric Light Co v. Holland, 6 RPC 243.
152. F.H. & B. Corporation v. Unichem Laboratories, AIR 1969 Bom 255; following Welsbach Incandescent Gas Light Co Ltd v. New Incandescent (Sunlight Patent) Gas Lighting Co Ltd 17 RPC 237.
153. Halsbury's Laws of England, 3rd edn, vol. 29, para. 123, quoted by J. Vimadlal in Farbewerke Hoechst A.G. v. Unichem Laboratories (1969) RPC 55 Bombay, H.C; see also Laxmi Dutt RupChand v. Nankau, AIR 1964 All.
154. See s. 3(c).
155. Beecham Group Ltd's (Amoxycillin) Appln. (1980) RPC 261 at 290. Bilcare Ltd. v. Amartara Pvt. Ltd. (2007) 34 PTC 419 (Del).
156. J. Graham, in Olin Mathieson Chemical Corporation v. Biorex Laboratories Ltd (1970) RPC 157 at 188 and in General Fire & Rubber Co v. Firestone Tyres & Rubber Co Ltd (1971) RPC 173 at 238; (1972) RPC at 497.
157. Welcome Foundation v. V.R. Laboratories (Australia) Pty Ltd (1982) RPC 343 at 346; Minnesota Mining & Mfg. Co v. Beiersdorf (Aust) Ltd (1980) FSR 449, both Australian cases.
158. 383 US 1 (1966).
159. V.K. Ahuja, Intellectual Property Rights in India, Second Edition, Lexis Nexis (2016) at p. 461.

130. To decide the question of obviousness, one may take into account, *inter alia*, such matters as:

(1) whether the invention has value and importance from a technical and commercial point of view;
(2) the history of the matter in so far as it may throw light on the obviousness or otherwise of the combination which has been claimed;
(3) the qualification which in the particular case the notional skilled workman must be presumed to have in approaching the problem;
(4) the nature of the problem itself; and
(5) the meaning of the words in the section that the invention claimed is obvious and does not involve any inventive step, having regard to what was known or used before the priority date of the claim in India.[160]

131. The test of obviousness will have to be decided only in a full-fledged trial.[161]

A combination may be said to be patentable where the component elements are so combined as to produce a new result or to arrive at an old result in a better or more expeditious or more economical manner. However, the mere bringing together of two or more things without some exercise of the inventive faculty in combining them is not subject matter for a patent. The inventor, in the case of a combination, may act on a number of principles that are well known, but if he/she experimented in order to see which combination produced a new and useful result and if he/she succeeds in ascertaining that such a result is arrived at by a particular combination, the combination will be considered for the grant of a patent.[162]

132. Since the definition of an invention includes an art or process of manufacture,[163] if the result of a new process is a new article, or a better article, or a cheaper article than that produced by old methods, the process is patentable. That is, provided that to arrive at such process, exercise of the inventive faculty was required.[164] It has also been held that a new and alternative method of arriving at the same result, irrespective of whether that result is better or cheaper, may be patentable.[165]

Section 3(d) of the Act requires that the discovery of a new form of a known substance has to result in the enhancement of the known efficacy. The idea behind section 3(d) is that it discourages evergreening and prevents such derivative or other forms of the already patented product being granted patent unless the derivatives or

160. See General Tire Co's case (1971) RPC 173 at 238; (1972) RPC 457.
161. Bajaj Auto v. TVS Motor (2008) 36 PTC 417 (Mad).
162. Lallubhai Chakubhai Jariwala v. Chimanlal Chunilal & Co, AIR 1936 Bom 99.
163. See s. 2(1)(j).
164. Crave v. Price, 1 Webst. P.C. 393 referred to in Alsop's Patent, 24 RPC 733 at 752.
165. It has been observed by the Controller General that generally a process is considered to be new if: (1) it results in a new product, or (2) it uses new starting materials, or (3) it employs a novel combination of steps even if such steps themselves may not be per se novel, Catalysts & Chemicals India (West Asia) Ltd v. Imperial Chemical Industries Ltd (1976) IPLR 84.

other forms differ significantly in properties with regard to efficacy.[166] The scope of 'known efficacy' under section 3(d) was elaborated in detail by the Supreme Court in *Novartis AG v. Union of India*,[167] wherein it was stated that:

> What is 'efficacy'? Efficacy means 'the ability to produce a desired or intended result'. Hence, the test of efficacy in the context of Section 3(d) would be different, depending upon the result the product under consideration is desired or intended to produce. In other words, the test of efficacy would depend upon the function, utility or the purpose of the product under consideration. Therefore, in the case of a medicine that claims to cure a disease, the test of efficacy can only be 'therapeutic efficacy'. The question then arises, what would be the parameter of therapeutic efficacy and what are the advantages and benefits that may be taken into account for determining the enhancement of therapeutic efficacy? With regard to the genesis of Section 3(d), and more particularly the circumstances in which Section 3(d) was amended to make it even more constrictive than before, we have no doubt that the 'therapeutic efficacy' of a medicine must be judged strictly and narrowly. Our inference that the test of enhanced efficacy in case of chemical substances, especially medicine, should receive a narrow and strict interpretation is based not only on external factors but there are sufficient internal evidence that leads to the same view. It may be noted that the text added to Section 3(d) by the 2005 amendment lays down the condition of 'enhancement of the known efficacy'. Further, the explanation requires the derivative to 'differ significantly in properties with regard to efficacy'. What is evident, therefore, is that not all advantageous or beneficial properties are relevant, but only such properties that directly relate to efficacy, which in case of medicine, as seen above, is its therapeutic efficacy.
>
> While dealing with the explanation it must also be kept in mind that each of the different forms mentioned in the explanation have some properties inherent to that form, e.g., solubility to a salt and hygroscopicity to a polymorph. These forms, unless they differ significantly in property with regard to efficacy, are expressly excluded from the definition of 'invention'. Hence, the mere change of form with properties inherent to that form would not qualify as 'enhancement of efficacy' of a known substance. In other words, the explanation is meant to indicate what is not to be considered as therapeutic efficacy.

Patents and Computer Programs

In February 2016, the Indian Patent Office amended its guidelines to provide clarity for patent examiners and practitioners on patenting computer-related inventions (CRIs). The Patent Office clarified that the substance of the invention must be evident outside of subject matter that is otherwise excluded from patentability.[168]

---

166. F. Hoffmann-La Roche Ltd. v. Cipla Limited (2009) 40 PTC 125 (Del).
167. (2013) 6 SCC 1.
168. Thomas Griffiths and Daniel Collopy, India releases new guidelines for computer-related inventions, LEXOLOGY (25 Feb. 2016), http://www.lexology.com/library/detail.aspx?g=a4711743-2eb5-45b2-b82a-7939e3f69a19.

Furthermore, the erstwhile Intellectual Property Appellate Board in 2020 allowed for the patent application on a 'method and device for accessing information sources and services on the web'.[169] This decision followed an order passed by Justice Pratibha Singh of the Delhi High Court which directed the patent office to re-examine the application in the context of the developments that have taken place since the filing of the original application.[170] The most notable development being the addition of the phrase per se in Section 3(k) of the Patents Act had previously barred computer programs from being patented. As stated in the CRI guidelines, this was done with the intent to ensure that inventions that are based on computer programs are patented and not the computer programs themselves. The only requirement being that the invention has to demonstrate a technical effect or a technical contribution, even if it is based on a computer program.

---

169. Allani Ferid v. Asst Controller of Patents & Designs OA/17/2020/PT/DEL.
170. Ferid Allani v. Union of India & Ors. W.P.(C) 7/2014 & CM APPL. 40736/2019.

Chapter 4. Formalities

133. Who may apply: An application for a patent may be made by any of the following persons:

(a) a person claiming to be the true and first inventor of the invention;
(b) the legal representative of the deceased person who immediately before his/her death was entitled to apply; and
(c) an assignee of the true and first inventor.[171]

Such an application may be made either individually or jointly with any other person.[172] The term 'true and the first inventor' means the inventor who first applied for a patent. It does not include either the first importer of an invention into India or a person to whom an invention is first communicated from outside India.[173] Where two persons have made the same invention independently and neither has used or disclosed it to the world, the one who applies for a patent first will be the true and first inventor, although the other may have invented it earlier in point of time.[174] In case a person contributed to one of the two main ideas of an invention, he/she would be considered as 'co-inventors'.[175]

134. As per section 2(1)(k) of the Act, 'legal representative' means a person who in law represents the estate of a deceased person. The right to apply for a patent, on the death of the owner of the right, devolves to his/her legal representative.

135. A corporation or a firm cannot be said to be an inventor,[176] as neither has the capacity to invent. However, they may be registered as patentees either on assignment by a patentee or jointly with the true and first inventor. Similarly, a financial partner cannot be treated as an inventor if he/she did not contribute towards the invention at all by way of technical knowledge or ingenuity or skill.[177]

136. The terms of a contract of employment, whether express or implied, between the employee and the employer, decide in each particular case whether the invention made by an employee should belong to the employer.[178] The mere existence of a contract of employment does not in any way disqualify an employee from getting a patent in his/her own name, unless the contract itself contained conditions that would compel him/her to communicate the benefits of his/her invention to those

171. Section 6(1).
172. Section 6(2).
173. Section 2(1)(y).
174. See Canadian General Electric Co v. Fada Radio Lt., AIR 1930 PC 1 at 5; followed in Bombay Agarwal Co v. Ramchand, AIR 1953 Nagpur 154 at 162, 163.
175. Norris' Patent (1988) RPC 159.
176. V.B. Mohammed Ibrahim v. Alfred Schafranek, AIR 1960 Mys 173 at 175.
177. V.B. Mohammad Ibrahim v. Alfred Schafranek, AIR 1960 Mys 173.
178. Statement of Law given in Frost's Patent Law & Practice, vol. 1, 21, quoted and approved by Lloyd-Jacob, J. in Charles Selz Ltd's Appln. 71 RPC 158 at 164. See also Marshall & Naylor's Patent, 17 RPC 553 at 555.

in whose employment he/she is.[179] This is regardless of whether he/she has used his/her employer's time and materials to complete his/her invention.[180]

137. The right to apply for a patent is assignable. The term 'assignee' includes an assignee of the assignee and the legal representative of a deceased assignee.[181] An assignee can be a natural person, or a legal person, i.e., a company, research organization or the Government.[182] An assignee of the person claiming to be the true and first inventor has the right to make an application for a patent under section 6(1)(b) of the Patents Act, 1970. As the Act or the rules thereunder do not lay down any formalities to be complied with while making the assignment, an oral assignment is not expressly disallowed. However, an assignment in writing is preferable.

138. An assignee's application for the grant of a patent should contain the name, address and nationality of the inventor.[183] An application to which the true and first inventor is not a party is void, and the irregularity cannot be cured by amendment.[184] The assignee should, along with the application, furnish proof of the right to make an application. In the alternative, such proof may be furnished within a period of six months from the date of making the application.[185]

139. Procedure: The Patent Rules, 1972, lay down the procedures to be followed while making an application, its examination in the Patent Office and other related matters. The forms to be used and the fees to be paid are listed in the Second Schedule and the First Schedule, respectively, to the Rules.

140. All applications should be filed at the appropriate office of the Patent Office as defined in Rule 4. The appropriate office of the Patent Office would depend on 'residence' or 'principal place of business', or the place from where the invention actually originated.[186]

141. An application for a patent must be made in the appropriate form and filed along with the prescribed fees.[187] The application should be in Form No. 1.[188] In order to simplify the procedure for payment of fees, the relevant provisions of the Patent Rules, 1972, were amended by the Patents Rules, 2003, which facilitates the payment of fees through electronic means apart from the conventional methods of cheque, bank draft and cash.

179. Patchett v. Sterling (1975) 72 RPC 50; Edisonia v. Forse (1908) 25 RPC 546.
180. Mellor v. William Beardmore & Co Ltd 44 RPC 175 at 191. See also Heald's application for Patent, 8 RPC 429 (an employer is not necessarily entitled to the benefit of an invention made by his servant).
181. Section 2(1)(ab).
182. Manual of Patent Office Practice and Procedure, March 2011 at p. 8.
183. See Form 1.
184. Edward Carter's Appln. 49 RPC 403 (application by a nominee of the inventor).
185. Section 7(2) and Rule 10.
186. Rule 4(1)(a).
187. Section 142(1) and Rule 7, along with Fourth Schedule.
188. See Rule 8 and Second Schedule.

142. Separate forms are prescribed for cases where the applicant is a true and first inventor, an assignee or a legal representative, or where it is a convention application or where the application is for a patent of addition. If the applicant is an assignee or legal representative, proof of the right to apply should be furnished along with the application or within six months from the date of filing the application.[189] However, in all cases, the application should contain the name of the person claiming to be the true and first inventor. If the applicant is not the true and first inventor, he/she should declare that he/she believes the person so named to be the true and first inventor, and the application should also state that the applicant is in possession of the invention.[190] Every application should be accompanied by a provisional or a complete specification.[191] A convention application should always be accompanied by the complete specification.[192] Each application should be confined to one invention only.[193] As per Rule 9, the application and other documents filed along with the application, if any, should be either in Hindi or English.

Section 8 provides for disclosure of information pertaining to foreign applications in respect of the same or substantially the same invention sought to be patented in India. The applicant has to file a statement providing the detailed particulars of such applications, as well as give an undertaking to the Controller. The undertaking includes that he/she would inform the Controller in writing if any other similar application is filed in another country within six months.[194] Courts have held that this is a mandatory provision, and the applicant is bound to furnish the required information.[195]

143. Specification: A description of the invention is called the 'specification'. A specification may be provisional or complete. The specification, whether provisional or complete, should describe the invention and should begin with a title sufficiently indicating the subject matter to which the invention relates.[196] It should contain the name, nationality and address of the applicant as given in the application and must be signed and dated by the applicant or his/her agent.[197] The specification should not contain any irrelevant matters which are not necessary for the elucidation of the invention.[198] If the specification is for a patent of addition, it should contain a specific reference to the number of the main patent, or of the application for the main patent, and also a definite statement that the invention comprises an improvement in, or a modification of, the main invention.[199]

---

189. Section 7(2) and Rule 10.
190. Section 7(3).
191. Section 7(4).
192. Section 136.
193. Section 7(1).
194. Rule 12.
195. Chemtura Corporation v. Union of India & Ors. (2009) 41 PTC 60 (Del); Cipla Ltd. v. F. Hoffman-La Roche Ltd. (2013) 54 PTC 217 (Del).
196. Section 10(1).
197. Rule 13(1).
198. Rule 13(5).
199. Rule 13(3).

144. Where an application is accompanied by a provisional specification, a complete specification should be filed within twelve months from the date of filing of the application. If the complete specification is not so filed, the application will be deemed to be abandoned. This privilege is not available to a convention application claiming convention priority, or to an application filed under the Patent Cooperation Treaty (PCT) designating India.[200] However, this period may be extended by three months, provided that a request for the same is made to the Controller and the prescribed fee paid on or before the date on which the complete specification is filed.[201] Where an application is accompanied by a complete specification, it may be treated as a provisional specification if the applicant so desires within twelve months from the date of application. The applicant must make a request for this purpose before the acceptance of the specification. This privilege is not available to a convention application claiming convention priority.[202]

145. A patent application shall be examined only upon the request of the applicant, and if no such request is made, the application shall be treated as withdrawn by the applicant.[203] Such request shall be made within forty-eight months of the date of application.[204] In case an application for the claim of a process patent is filed before 1 January 2005, the request shall also be made within forty-eight months from the date of filing the application. At the application stage, the Controller sifts through the applications, and the benefit of doubt, if any, is given to the applicant. An application will only be refused if it cannot be said to be within the ambit of the Act. There will be, in view of the presumption in favour of the application at this stage, very few cases where the Controller will take the extreme step of refusal, but in a proper case, he/she is bound to do so. If he/she is wrong, his/her decision can be reversed on appeal.[205]

146. On the filing of a complete specification, an application will be examined by an examiner in respect of the following:

- Whether the application and specification comply with requirements of the Act and the Rules made thereunder, as to both formal and substantive matters.
- Whether there is any lawful ground of objection to the grant of a patent under the Act.
- Whether, under section 13, there is anticipation by prior publication and prior claim in the records of the Patent Office. However, as per section 18(3), the investigation under section 13 is not conclusive on the question of anticipation, and an objection based on prior claim can be raised even if it is not cited by the Examiner.
- Any other matter that may be prescribed.[206]

200. Section 9(1).
201. Section 9(2) proviso, Form 5 and item 5 of the First Schedule.
202. Section 9(3). There is no special form prescribed for making the request.
203. Section 11B read with Rule 24B(1)(i) and Form 18.
204. Rule 24B (1)(i).
205. L'Oreal's Appln. (1970) RPC 565.
206. Section 12(1).

147. The Examiner will ordinarily submit his/her report to the Controller within the period prescribed from the date when the matter was referred to him/her for examination.[207] Rule 24B(1)(ii) specifies that the examiner shall make the report ordinarily within one month but not exceeding three months. Section 13 further provides that examination and investigations envisaged under section 12 or section 13 do not warrant the validity of any patent, and no liability shall be incurred by the Central Government or its officers in this regard. Thus, grant of patent does not guarantee the validity of such patent.[208]

148. If the Controller so requires, drawings should be supplied for the purposes of any provisional or complete specification, and they should be prepared in accordance with Rule 15.[209] Models or samples, where required by the Controller under section 10(3), should be furnished in accordance with Rule 16.

149. An application for a patent should be confined to one invention only.[210] A complete specification must also, therefore, relate to a single invention. The Controller has a duty to refuse an application relating to more than one invention at any stage before the grant of the patent.[211] However, the validity of the patent cannot be by a person in legal proceedings on the ground that it has been granted for more than one invention.[212]

150. The applicant has to comply with the requirements of the patent office, within the prescribed period from the date on which the first statement of objection was forwarded by the Controller, failing which the application will be deemed to have been abandoned.[213] Where the application, specification, or any document filed in connection with the application is returned to the applicant for meeting some requirements, the amended documents should be re-filed within the prescribed period, failing which the application will be deemed not to have complied with the requirements, unless the applicant can show to the satisfaction of the Controller that the re-filing did not take place due to reasons beyond the applicant's control.[214]

151. Once the complete specification is accepted, the Controller will allot a serial number to the application, which will be the number of the patent so granted.[215]

---

207. Section 12(2).
208. M/s Standipack Pvt. Ltd. v. Oswal Trading Co. Ltd, AIR 2000 Del 23; J. Mitra and Co. Pvt. Ltd. v. Kesar Mendicants and Anr. (2008) 36 PTC 568 (Del).
209. Section 10(2) and Rule 15.
210. Section 7(1).
211. Mobiloil Corporation's Appln. (1969) RPC 586 at 597 (PAT).
212. Section 46(2).
213. Section 21(1). In Elkem-Spigerverket A/s v. Controller General of Patents, 2 DPD 498 (Writ Petition), the order of the Controller General treating an application as deemed to have been abandoned under s. 21 was set aside as no notice was given to the applicant and no opportunity given to them for showing cause. Explanation to s. 21(1). See also Pensalt Chemicals Corporation's Appln. (1968) RPC 27.
214. Ibid.
215. Rule 37.

152. An application or a specification cannot be published by the Controller except with the consent of the applicant, till the expiration of the period prescribed under section 11(A), or till such time it is opened for public inspection under section 43, or unless it is an application for leave to amend an application for a patent or a complete specification or a document relating thereto, made after the grant of patent, as provided for under section 57(3).[216] However, in case of inventions subject to secrecy under the provisions of sections 35–42, contained in Chapter VII, no publication or inspection of the specification is permitted even with the consent of the applicant.[217]

153. Amendment of application and specification: Rules 81–83 lay down the procedure for amendment of an application or a complete specification of a patent under section 57. An application for amendment must be filed in Form 13 and should contain a statement of the nature of the amendment and the reasons for which the amendment is sought.[218]

154. The application for amendment and the nature of the proposed amendment may be published, where the application for amendment is made after grant of the patent. The Controller will also notify all persons who, in his/her opinion, may have an interest in the matter.[219] Any person interested may give notice of opposition to the application in Form 14 within three months from the date of advertisement in the Official Gazette. Any amendment that is allowed will be advertised in the Official Gazette.[220]

155. Convention application: If a person has made an application for a patent in a convention country,[221] and if he/she or his/her assignee or legal representative makes an application in respect of the same invention in India within twelve months from the date of the application in the convention country, he/she or his/her assignee or legal representative will get the benefit of the priority date of his/her application made in the convention country.[222] In case an applicant wishes to avail the benefit of priority given to a convention application under section 135, he/she should apply in the appropriate form, that is, Form No. 2. The application should be filed within twelve months from the date on which the basic application was made. Where there are more than one foreign application involved, the period of twelve months should begin from the date of the earliest of such applications.[223] The application should be accompanied by a complete specification and should contain the particulars

216. Section 143, as amended by Patents (Amendment) Act, 2005.
217. See the opening words of s. 143, 'Subject to the provisions of Chapter VII'.
218. Section 57(2).
219. Section 57(3) and Rules 81–83.
220. Rule 83.
221. See s. 135.
222. Section 135.
223. Section 135(1).

specified in section 136. Convention priority will not be granted to a document containing merely a reference to the application filed in a convention country or identification by number thereof.[224] Applications filed under the PCT designating India: If an application is filed under the PCT (designating India) in relation to the same subject matter as an application filed previously in India, the provisions of section 135(1) and 135(2) will apply.[225]

156. Only the person who has filed the 'basic application', or the legal representative, or the assignee of that person can file a convention application. The words 'without prejudice to the provisions contained in section 6' mean without detriment to the applicants' right to file an ordinary application under section 6.[226]

157. If the inventor desires to have his/her name mentioned as the inventor in a patent, he/she may make an application to that effect, before the grant of the patent. The reference to any person as an inventor will not confer or derogate any rights under the patent.[227] Where an inventor has been mentioned, any other person, who alleges that the former ought not to have been so mentioned, may apply to the Controller any time for a certificate to that effect. The Controller may, after hearing any person who may be interested, issue such a certificate.[228]

158. Grant of a patent: Where an application for a patent has been found to be in order for grant of the patent and the Controller has not refused the application or the application is not in contravention of the Act, the patent has to be granted as expeditiously as possible to the applicant, with the seal of the patent office. The date on which the patent is granted must be entered in the register.[229]

159. Date of sealing: The date of grant of patent is material for calculating the period for filing an application for compulsory licence[230] and for a 'licenses of right' endorsement.[231]

160. Date of patent: The patent will bear the date on which the application for patent was filed.[232] The purpose of 'date of patent' is to calculate the duration of the patent and for reckoning the time for payment of renewal fee.[233] The date of the patent will be entered in the register.

---

224. See Temescal Metallurgical Corporation's Appln. (1964) RPC 1, approving R's Appln., 56 RP, C 160.
225. Section 135(3).
226. Metallurical Processes Ltd and I.S.C. Smelting Ltd's Appln. 1 DPD 39 at 49 (Patent Office).
227. Section 28(1), read with s. 28(4).
228. Section 28(7).
229. Section 43.
230. Section 84(1).
231. Section 86(1).
232. Section 45(1), Bajaj Auto Ltd. v. TVS Motor Company (2008) (36) PTC 417 (Mad).
233. See s. 53 read with Rule 80.

161. Determining the date of patent as per section 45(1) is subject to certain other provisions of the Act. The other provisions that affect the date of patent are:

- Section 9(3): where a complete specification filed along with the application has been treated as a provisional one.
- Explanation to section 16: ante-dating of the complete specification, necessitated by a division of application where the invention is related to more than one invention.
- Section 17(2): post-dating of the complete specification by order of the Controller when the specification has been amended to comply with the requirements of the office under section 15.
- Sections 54 and 55: the date of a patent of addition is determined by the date of the patent in respect of the main invention.

162. A patent will be granted in the form specified in the Third Schedule and will bear the number allotted to the application under Rule 37.[234]

163. As per the provisions of section 52, where a patent has been revoked under section 64 on the ground that it was obtained wrongfully and in contravention of the rights of the petitioner, the court or Appellate Board may permit grant of the patent to the petitioner instead of revoking the patent. If, however, it is found that only some claims have been wrongly obtained, the court instead of revoking the patent may direct the amendment of the specification and permit the grant of such part of the invention that has been wrongly obtained by the patentee, to the petitioner.[235] An application for the grant of a patent, as ordered by the High Court, must be made in Form 12 within three months from the date of the order. The application should be accompanied by a statement of facts on which the petitioner relies and the relief claimed, along with a certified copy of the order of the court. The time taken for obtaining a certified copy of the order will be excluded in calculating the period of three months.[236] No suit shall be brought for any infringement of a patent granted under section 52 before the actual date on which such patent was granted.[237]

234. Section 46 and Rule 74.
235. Section 52(1).
236. Rule 79.
237. Section 52(3).

Chapter 5. Ownership and Transfer (Assignment: Licences)

164. A patentee's right to the exclusive use of a patented invention, as per provisions of the Act, is a right to property.[238] The rights of patentee are negative rights, which are enforceable at the instance of the patent holder. The grant of patent confers the following rights:[239]

(1) Where the subject matter of the patent is a product, the exclusive right to prevent third parties, without his/her consent, from the act of making, using, selling or importing for those purposes that product in India.
(2) Where the subject matter of the patent is a process, the exclusive right to prevent third parties, without his/her consent, from the act of using that process and from the act of using, selling or importing for those purposes the product obtained directly by that process in India.[240]

The original patentee can transfer this right to any other person by assignment. This right may also be transferred by operation of law. The right to property in a patent is a statutory creation. There is no such thing as a common law right to property in a patent. The laws governing transfer of a patent are therefore determined by statute.

165. Transfer: The patentee has the exclusive right by him/herself, his/her agents or licensees to make, use, exercise, sell or distribute the patented article. A patentee can transfer any one or more of these rights, either wholly or partly, to any other person.[241] A patentee is empowered to assign, grant licences under, or otherwise deal with the patent for any consideration. Where the patentee is a co-owner of the patent, he/she can assign any share of the patent or grant licences only with the consent of the co-owners[242] or as per directions of the Controller.[243] The power to transfer patent rights is also subject to any rights vested in any other person of which notice is entered in the register.[244] Any equity in respect of a patent may be enforced in the same way as any other movable property.[245]

166. A contract relating to the sale or lease of a patented article may contain restrictive conditions regarding the purchase or use of non-patented articles. Such conditions will be void.[246] Any contract for the sale, lease or licence of a patented

238. Farben fabrieken Bayer A.G. v. Joint Controller of Patents and Designs AIR 1963 Cal 433; 67 CWN 743; Telemecanique & Controls (I) Limited v. Schneider Electric Industries SA (2002) 24 PTC 632 (Del); F. Hoffman-La Roche Ltd. v. Cipla Limited (2008) 37 PTC 71 (Del).
239. Section 48.
240. Bayer Corporation & Anr. v. Union of India & Ors. (2013) 43 PTC 12 (Del); F. Hoffman-La Roche Ltd. v. Cipla Limited (2008) 37 PTC 71 (Del).
241. Section 70.
242. Section 50(3).
243. Section 51.
244. Section 70, See also s. 69 dealing with registration of assignments, etc.
245. Proviso to s. 70.
246. Section 140.

article may be terminated at any time after the patent has ceased to be in force, by the purchaser or lessee, by giving three months' notice to the other party.[247]

167. Transfer of any interest in a patent, including an assignment, mortgage or licence will be valid only if the following requirements are met:

– the assignment, mortgage or licence should be in writing, drawn up in the form of a document embodying all the terms and conditions governing the rights and obligations between the parties; and duly executed.[248]

168. For the creation of any interest in a patent, whether it is by way of an assignment, mortgage or licence, registration of the document creating such an interest is necessary as per the provisions of section 68. The document must contain all the terms and conditions governing the parties' rights and obligations. Any one party to the contract may file an application for registration. The procedure for registration of an assignment, transmission, mortgage or licence of a patent is stated in section 69 and Rules 90–92. The Controller will enter in his/her register, upon being satisfied as to proof of title, the person entitled to the patent as the proprietor or co-proprietor of the patent, as the case may be. Any other interest in the patent that the person is entitled to will also be entered into the register. The Controller should be given copies of all agreements, licences and other documents affecting the title to the patent or any licence thereunder.[249]

The Controller or any court will not admit a document in respect of which no entry has been made in the register (except in a rectification proceeding), as evidence of title of any person to a patent, unless otherwise directed. The Controller or the court will record the reasons for their directions in writing.[250]

169. Assignments: There are three kinds of assignments:

(1) Legal assignment.
(2) Equitable assignment.
(3) Mortgages.

170. Although the term 'assignment' is not defined by the Act, it means an act whereby the patentee wholly or partly transfers all patent rights to the assignee, who then acquires the right to prevent others from making, using, exercising, or vending the invention. The patentee may assign the whole patent or any part of it for the whole of India or for a part thereof. An assignee includes the legal representative of a deceased assignee.[251] A firm/corporation can also apply for a patent as an

247. Section 141.
248. See s. 68.
249. Rules 90–92.
250. Section 69(5), Sergi Transformer Explosion Prevention Technologies Pvt. Ltd. v. Kumar Pratap Anil (2014) 58 PTC 449 (Del).
251. Section 2(1)(ab) and (k).

assignee.[252] Where the assignee consists of two or more persons, they become co-owners of the patent and their rights are governed by the provisions of section 50.

The right to apply for a patent for an invention may also be assigned.[253]

171. Legal assignment means an assignment or an agreement to assign an existing patent by a deed.

172. Equitable assignment takes place where the intention to assign is evident, although no formality may have taken place. In other words, where the patentee agrees to give another person a certain defined share of the patent with immediate effect, through any document including a letter, it is an equitable assignment. Although an equitable assignee cannot have his/her name entered in the register as proprietor of the patent, he/she may nevertheless have notice of his/her interest entered in the register. An assignment of patent rights by an applicant before the grant of the patent is an equitable assignment.[254]

173. Assignment by mortgage is said to take place when the patentee/mortgagor executes a document transferring his/her rights in the patent, wholly or partly, to the mortgagee with a view to securing the payment of a sum of money. On repaying the sum of money, the patentee/mortgagor becomes entitled to have the patent transferred back to him/her. Although the mortgagee will not be entitled to have his/her name entered in the register as proprietor of the patent, he/she may have notice of his/her interest as mortgagee entered in the register.

174. Transfer by operation of law: When a patentee dies or becomes bankrupt and in the case of a company, when it is dissolved, any patent registered in its name is said to be transferred by operation of law, in the same manner as any other form of property. Laws applicable to ownership and devolution of movable property will apply. The person who thereby becomes entitled to the patent has to apply to the Controller for registration of his/her title.

175. Acquisition by Central Government: The Central Government is empowered under the provisions of section 102 to acquire a patent from the patentee, or an invention which is the subject of an application for a patent from the applicant, for a public purpose.

176. Licences: A licence granted by the patentee permits any other person or persons to make, use, or exercise the invention, which would otherwise be illegal for them to do.[255] The following licences may be granted: implied, express, statutory,

---

252. Shining Industries v. Shri Krishna Industries, AIR 1975 All 231.
253. Section 7(2).
254. Gillette Safety Razor Co Ltd v. A.W. Gamage Ltd, RPC 492 at 499; Bowden's Patents Syndicate Ltd v. Smith & Co, 21 RPC 438 at 443.
255. Heap v. Hartley, 6 RPC 495.

exclusive, non-exclusive or limited. For a licence to be valid, it has to be in writing, and an application has to be filed with the Controller for registration of the licensing agreement.[256]

177. A purchaser of a patent for value, without notice of any conditions attached to the patentee's title, has a legal title and could give a good title to a purchaser from him/her even with notice of such conditions. On the other hand, an equitable assignee takes, generally speaking, no better title than his/her assignor.[257]

178. A patentee, in an action relating to the assignment of, or the granting of a licence in relation to a patent, is, under certain circumstances, estopped from attacking the validity of the patent in question. This is based on the principle that a grantor cannot defeat his/her own grant.[258] Further, if a patentee guarantees the validity of a patent in an agreement to sell the patent, the assignee can set up the plea of invalidity of the patent in a suit arising from the agreement.[259] A licensee, however, cannot challenge the validity of a patent in an action under the licence because in such cases the title is not in issue. A licensee does not have any ownership rights over the patent, only a licence to work a patent.[260] Exceptions to this rule are circumstances where it can be proved that facts which deprived the invention of its validity were fraudulently suppressed by the patentee.[261]

179. Assignment of Licence and Sub-Licensing: A simple licence to work a patent may not be assignable. However, if there is any evidence to show that there was an intention that the licence should not be limited exclusively to the immediate licensee, then such a licence may be assigned.[262]

256. Section 68, National Research and Development Corporation of India v. Delhi Cloth and General Mills, AIR 1980 Del 132.
257. Actien Gesellschaft Cartonnager Industrie v. Temler & Seeman, 18 RPC 6.
258. Franklain Hocking & Co Ltd v. Franklin Hocking, 4 RPC 255; 6 RPC 69 (HL).
259. Nadel v. Martin, 23 RPC 41 (HL), followed in Henderson v. Shields, 24 RPC 108.
260. Adie v. Clark (1876) Ch D 134 (CA), as interpreted in Fuel Economy Co Ltd v. Murray, 47 RPC 346.
261. Cummings v. Stewart, 30 RPC 1.
262. Bower v. Hodges, 22 LJ (CP) 194, followed in Lawson v. Donald Macpherson & Co Ltd, 14 RPC 696.

Chapter 6. Scope of Exclusive Rights

180. A patent is a statutory means of granting certain monopoly rights to a patentee for a specified period, subject to certain conditions. The monopoly rights include the right to make, use and sell the patented article or process. The consequence of the patentee having exclusive rights is that he/she can prevent all others from making or using the patented article or using the patented process. A patent is considered a species of property that is capable of being owned and transferred like any other property. A patentee also has the power to assign the patent, grant licences under, or otherwise deal with it for any consideration. All these statutory rights are subject to various conditions and limitations.

181. It may be noted that a patent does not give the patentee any right to use or manufacture the invention. This is a right that he/she would have had even if there was no patent at all. The only difference in the absence of a patent would be that the entire world would also have the same right. What the patent confers is the right to exclude others from manufacturing in a particular way and using a particular invention.[263]

182. Right to use and exercise the patent: Section 48 confers on the patentee the exclusive right to make, use, exercise, sell or distribute the patented article or substance in India, or to use or exercise the method or process if the patent is for a process. This right can be exercised either by the patentee him/herself or by his/her agents or licensees. Section 48 states very clearly that the rights granted under the section are subject to the other provisions of the Act.

183. When a patent is granted to two or more persons, the co-owners are individually entitled to an equal and undivided share in the patent.[264] Each of them is entitled, by him/herself or his/her agents, to make, use or exercise the patent without accounting to the others.[265] A co-owner of a patent cannot assign any share in the patent or grant a licence without the consent of the other co-owners.[266] However, all these provisions are subject to any agreement to the contrary between the parties. The law applicable to the ownership and devolution of moveable property shall apply to patents. The mutual rights or obligations of trustees or of the legal representatives of the deceased person or their rights and obligations are not affected by section 50.[267]

---

263. Steers v. Rogers, 10 RPC 245 (HL); Telemecanique & Controls (I) Limited v. Schneider Electric Industries SA (2002) 24 PTC 632 (Del); F. Hoffman-La Roche Ltd. v. Cipla Limited (2008) 37 PTC 71 (Del).
264. Section 50(1).
265. Section 50(2).
266. Section 50(3).
267. Section 50(5).

184. The applicant for a patent can exercise all the privileges and rights of a patentee, except the filing of a suit for infringement during the period from the date of advertisement of the acceptance of a complete specification and the date of sealing of the patent.

185. The rights conferred on a patent of addition are the same as those conferred on other patents, except those provided by sections 54–56.

Chapter 7. Limitations and Exceptions to the Scope of Patent Protection

186. The basic objective of the Act in granting patents is to encourage inventions and to secure that the inventions are worked in India on a commercial scale[268] and to the fullest extent without undue delay. The rationale is that the patented invention should be worked on a commercial scale to ensure that the benefit reaches the largest number of people.[269] The Act also seeks that the protection and enforcement of patent rights contribute to the promotion of technological innovation and to the transfer and dissemination of technology. It acts in the mutual advantage of producers and users of technological knowledge and in a manner conducive to social and economic welfare and to a balance of rights and obligations. The patentee is sought to be discouraged from exploiting the invention for his/her sole use. The remedies adopted under the present Patents Act against abuse of patent rights include defining the purpose of granting patents, providing for a system of compulsory licensing by the Controller under specified circumstances, the use of inventions for the purposes of Government and revocation of the patent for non-working.

§1. Compulsory Licences

187. The Controller may grant compulsory licences upon an application being made under section 84 to the Controller by an interested person on grounds specified therein. The applicant in this case must make out a prima facie case, as required under section 87, whereupon notice of the same shall be issued to the patentee and shall also be published in the Official Journal.

Thereafter, if the Controller is satisfied, the compulsory licence may be granted, as per the provisions of section 88. The licence may be subject to terms and conditions under section 90.

188. A compulsory licence to work a patented invention may be granted under section 84 by the Controller to an interested person on one of the following grounds:

- the reasonable requirements of the public with respect to the patented invention have not been satisfied; or
- the patented invention is not available to the public at a reasonable price; or
- the patented invention has not worked in the territory of India.

189. The Controller is not bound to take into account any matter subsequent to the making of the application for a compulsory licence. However, the controller can consider an application for a compulsory licence only after the expiry of three years from the date of grant of the patent. It may be noted that for the purpose of granting

268. Glaverbal S.A. v. Dave Rose & Ors. (2010) 43 PTC 630 (Del).
269. Bayer Corporation & Anr. v. Union of India & Ors. (2013) 43 PTC 12 (Del).

compulsory licence, or endorsement with the words 'licenses of right', or revocation of patent for non-working, the term 'patentee' includes an exclusive licensee as well.[270]

In *Bayer Corporation v. Union of India*,[271] the Bombay High Court held that 'an application for compulsory licence can be made by any person to the Controller on satisfaction of the following two per-requirements/conditions:

(a) An application for compulsory licence can be made only after expiration of three years from the date of the grant of patent to the patent holder; and
(b) The applicant should have made an effort to obtain a voluntary licence of the patented invention from the patent holder on reasonable terms and conditions.

It is only on the satisfaction of the above two requirements that the Controller can consider the application for compulsory licence'.

190. Under section 84, failure to satisfy the reasonable requirements of the public may arise from the following causes:

- inadequate manufacture in India or failure to grant licences on reasonable terms;
- non-working of the patent in India on a commercial scale;
- conditions imposed by the patentee upon the grant of licence;
- demand for the patented article being met by importation from abroad; and
- commercial working of the patented invention in India being hindered or prevented by import of the patented articles from abroad.[272]

191. Thus, if there was no actual working of the patent in India at the time of the application, and the patentee arranged for subsequent working probably for the purpose of defeating the application, it was not acceptable as a defence against granting a licence. Where, however, the patentee has taken with promptitude adequate or reasonable steps to start the working of the invention in India on a commercial scale, the Controller may take this into consideration.[273]

192. Where an application for a compulsory licence is made under section 84, the Controller should exercise his/her powers with a view to secure the following:

- that patented inventions are worked on a commercial scale in India without undue delay and to the fullest extent that is reasonably practicable; and
- that the interests of any person for the time being working or developing an invention in India under the protection of a patent are not unfairly prejudiced.[274]

---

270. Section 82(b).
271. 2014(60)PTC277(Bom).
272. Section 84(7).
273. Section 91(2).
274. Section 89.

193. However, securing the fulfilment of both the clauses may sometimes lead to conflict of interests to be reconciled. If the Controller is satisfied that either of the grounds referred to in section 84(1) has been established, then he/she may order the patentee to grant a licence upon such terms as he/she may deem fit.[275]

194. Any person interested in working the invention may make an application for the grant of a compulsory licence. However, the Controller also has to assess the technical skill and the financial resources of the applicant to arrive at a decision. The decision ascertains whether the applicant has the ability to work the invention to public advantage or whether the applicant has made efforts to obtain a licence from the patentee on reasonable terms and conditions.[276] No licence is required for using the patented invention merely for the purpose of experiment, research or imparting instructions to pupils.[277] A person who is already the holder of a licence may also make an application for a compulsory licence.

195. The applicant for a compulsory licence has to make out a prima facie case[278] as to why a compulsory licence should be granted to him/her since he/she is the one alleging that reasonable requirements of the public with respect to the patented invention have not been satisfied. The Controller may refuse the application if a prima facie case has not been made out. This is the import of section 87(1) read with Rule 97. The Controller will order the patentee to grant a licence only if one of the grounds specified in section 84(1) is established to his/her satisfaction, and the Controller will proceed with the application under section 87 only where the applicant has made out a prima facie case for the making of an order. Only if the applicant has made out a prima facie case will the patentee be called upon to reply to the application.[279] Section 87 lays down the procedure whereby the patentee or any other person interested, as specified in the register, may oppose the application for the compulsory licence.

196. Section 90 specifies the terms and conditions of a compulsory licence, wherein the Controller shall endeavour to secure that:

(1) royalty and other remuneration to be paid to the patent holder should be reasonable, having regard to the nature of the invention, the expenditure incurred by the patent holder in making and developing the patent;
(2) the patented invention is worked to the fullest extent by the person to whom the compulsory licence is granted with reasonable profit to him;
(3) the patented articles are made available to the public at a reasonably affordable price; and

275. Section 84(5).
276. Section 84(6).
277. Section 47(3). This rule applies only to patents granted under the present Act. There is no statutory authority to use a patent for the purpose of experiment or research under the Act of 1911.
278. Bayer Corporation v. Union of India 2014(60)PTC277(Bom).
279. Section 87.

(4) the licence granted to the applicant would be a non-exclusive licence and non-assignable.

The basic objective of granting a compulsory licence is to prevent the patentee from not fulfilling the reasonable requirements of the public, not those of particular individuals. The inability to supply the patented article or refusal to grant a licence to a particular individual would not necessarily amount to default in supplying the patented article or refusal to grant licences within the meaning of section 90. Therefore, to establish a case for compulsory licence, the applicant will have to prove not only default towards him/herself but also default towards the public in general.[280] Since the provisions of section 84 are mainly for the benefit and protection of the public, the Controller or the court will look first to the interest of the public and not to that of the individual.

Section 91 provides that at any time after the sealing of a patent, any person who has the right to work any other patented invention either as patentee or as licence thereof, exclusive or otherwise, may apply to the Controller for the grant of a licence of the first patent. He/she can apply on the ground that he/she is prevented or hindered without such licence from working the other invention efficiently or to the best advantage possible.[281]

§2. Compulsory Licences on Notification by the Central Government

197. If the Central Government is satisfied that in respect of any patent or class of patents, compulsory licences should be granted in the public interest to work the invention at any time after sealing, it may make a declaration to the effect in the Official Gazette. The effect of such declaration will be that the Controller will grant licences in respect of such patents, to any person interested, in an application being made to him/her. In settling the terms of the licence, the Controller will endeavour to secure that the articles made under the patent shall be available to the public at the lowest prices, consistent with the patentee deriving a reasonable advantage from the patent rights. Under section 92, the Central Government upon being satisfied that a compulsory licence be granted upon a patent because of the circumstances arising out of national emergency/extreme urgency/public non-commercial use, then it shall grant such licence at any time after the grant of the patent.[282] If the controller feels that because of national emergency, extreme urgency and public non-commercial uses, which include cases like AIDS, tuberculosis, malaria, epidemics, he shall immediately grant a compulsory licence without following the procedures provided under the Act. This beneficial provision can be really helpful in the case of emergencies. This section is based on the principles enshrined under Article 31 of TRIPS which enables the member countries to allow the patent for use by the

280. Robin Electric Lamp Co Ltd's Appln. 32 RPC 202.
281. F. Hoffman-La Roche Ltd. & Anr. v. Cipla Ltd. (2012) 52 PTC 1 (Del).
282. With the first compulsory licence being granted in 2012 for Bayer's Drug Nexawar. See Shamnad Basheer, Breaking News: India's First Compulsory License Granted!, SPICY IP (12 Mar. 2012) https://spicyip.com/2012/03/breaking-news-indias-first-compulsory.html.

government, or third parties authorized by the government. Such authorization should be considered on individual merits. Doha Declaration of 2001 emphasized the need to address public health issues around the world, especially in developing nations.

However, given that the Patents Act does not provide for the definition of terms such as 'circumstance of national emergency' and 'a circumstance of extreme urgency', the courts would be required to interpret these expressions on a case-by-case basis. One situation where the application of the compulsory licensing provisions was being advocated for was in 2020–2021 during the outbreak of the COVID-19 virus. Those in support of it saw its usage as a critical tool in addressing the issue of vaccine inequity.[283]

Section 92(A) provides for grant of compulsory licensees for the export of patented pharmaceutical products in certain exceptional circumstances. Under this provision, compulsory licence shall be available for manufacture and export of patented pharmaceutical products to any country having insufficient or no manufacturing capacity in the pharmaceutical sector for the concerned product to address public health problems. This is subject to the condition that compulsory licence has been granted by such country or such country has, by notification or otherwise, allowed importation of the patented pharmaceutical products from India.

Termination of compulsory licence is provided in section 94 on an application of the patentee or any other person deriving interest from the patent if the Controller is satisfied that the circumstances that gave rise to the grant of compulsory licence no longer exist. In considering such a termination application, the Controller will hear the licensee and ensure that the rights of the licensee are not unduly prejudiced.

§3. Use of Invention in Foreign Vessels or Foreign Aircraft

198. The use of a patented article beyond the three-mile limit of territorial waters is not an infringement within jurisdiction.[284] Furthermore, the use of a patented invention in a foreign vessel or aircraft or land vehicle which temporarily or accidentally happens to be within the country's jurisdiction is not deemed to be an infringement of the patent.[285] It is necessary that the invention must be used in the body of the vessel or in the machinery, tackle, apparatus or other accessories thereof on board the vessel and for its actual needs only; or in the case of aircraft or land

283. Arul Scaria & Vikas Kathuria, Compulsory License under Patent and Competition Law to Ensure Vaccine Equity, ORF (3 May 2021) https://www.orfonline.org/expert-speak/compulsory-license-under-patent-and-competition-law-to-ensure-vaccine-equity/. There were also concerns about the fact that deployment of compulsory licensing would not result in access to vaccines, as there were uncertainties if there was actually a patented vaccine and whether in the absence of technical know-how can these vaccines be re-engineered at scale and quickly. See Tamali Sen Gupta & Dhruv Shekhar, COVID Pandemic and Intellectual Property Rights, BW Legal World (9 Jun. 2021) http://bwlegalworld.businessworld.in/article/COVID-Pandemic-and-Intellectual-Property-Rights/09-06-2021-392419/.

284. V.D. Ltd v. Boston Deep Sea Fishing & Ice Co Ltd 52 RPC 303 at 331; relying on Newall v. Elliott, 10 Jurist NS 954.

285. Section 49.

vehicle, in the construction or working of such aircraft or vehicle or of the accessories thereof. However, the exemption from infringement does not apply to vessels, aircraft or land vehicles owned by persons ordinarily resident in a foreign country, the laws of which do not confer corresponding rights with respect to the use of inventions in vessels, aircraft or land vehicles owned by residents in India.

Chapter 8. Duration of Protection: Maintenance and Termination of Patent Protection

§1. Duration

199. A patent is granted for a limited period of time. Section 53 specifies the law with regard to the term of a patent. After the Patents (Amendment) Act, 2002, the term of every patent which has not expired and has not ceased to have effect on the date of commencement of such Act shall be twenty years from the date of filing of the application for the patent. In case of international applications filed under the PCT designating India, the term of the patent shall be twenty years from the international filing date accorded under the PCT.

200. The patentee has to periodically renew the patent by paying the prescribed fee before the patent lapses; otherwise, it ceases to have any force. Upon the cessation of the patent, due to non-payment of renewal fee or on the completion of the patent term, the subject matter of the patent loses all protection and becomes part of the public domain.[286]

§2. Revocation and Surrender of Patents

201. A patent is granted only upon the fulfilment of several conditions. If these conditions are not fulfilled, a patent may be revoked. Section 64 sets out grounds on which a patent may be revoked. A patent may be revoked for any of the following reasons:

- the patent was obtained wrongfully;
- the subject matter of the claim is not an invention;
- the invention was claimed in a valid claim of an earlier priority date contained in the complete specification of another patent granted in India;
- the patent is of no utility;
- the patent was granted on the application of a person not entitled to apply;
- the applicant obtained the patent by furnishing false information;[287]
- the invention is obvious or does not involve any inventive step;[288]
- the invention is not new;
- the complete specification does not sufficiently and fairly describe the invention and the manner in which it is to be worked;
- the leave to amend the complete specification was obtained by fraud;
- the applicant did not abide by directions of secrecy relating to an invention relevant to defence purposes; or
- the invention was secretly used in India.

286. Section 53(4).
287. Chemura Corporation v. Union of India & ors. (2009) 41 PTC 260 (Del).
288. F. Hoffman-La Roche Ltd. & Anr. v. Cipla Ltd. (2012) 52 PTC 1 (Del).

202. Section 64 provides that the patent may be revoked on a petition of 'any person interested'[289] or of the Central Government by the IPAB. It can also be revoked on a counterclaim in a suit for infringement by the High Court. A 'person interested' within the meaning of section 64 refers to a person who has a direct, present and tangible commercial interest which is injured or affected by the continuance of the patent on the register.[290]

As per the provisions of section 65, if the Central Government is satisfied that the grant of patent is for an invention relating to atomic energy, it may direct the Controller to revoke the patent. This is to enforce the provisions of section 20(1) of the Atomic Energy Act, 1962. The Controller will give notice to the patentee and other persons whose names are entered in the register. He/she will also give the parties an opportunity for being heard. The Controller, revoking the patent, may permit an amendment of the specification.

203. Furthermore, as per the provisions of section 66, the Central Government may suo moto revoke a patent in public interest if in its opinion the patent or the mode in which it is exercised is mischievous to the State or generally prejudicial to the public. The patentee will be given an opportunity of being heard before the revocation. A declaration to the effect will be made in the Official Gazette, and thereupon, the patent will be deemed revoked. Revocation of a patent under section 66 is final and is not appealable.

204. The Controller, on an application from the Central Government or any other person interested, may revoke the patent for non-working. This is as per the provisions of section 85 of the Act. In recent years, sustained efforts by Dr Shamnad Basheer have led to courts directing patent working disclosure requirements to be taken up seriously.[291] In the same matter, the Delhi High Court held that licensing and sublicensing requirements of patents are not confidential documents as all information regarding the grant of patent is already available on the website of the Patents Office. These disclosures are to be made through Form 27 as mandated by section 146 of the Patents Act read with Rule 131 of the Patent Rules, 2003.

205. In addition to the above, under section 64(4), the Central Government may petition the High Court to revoke a patent on the ground that the patentee has failed to comply with its request to use the patented invention for purposes of Government, and if the High Court is satisfied that the patentee has without reasonable cause failed to comply with the request of the Central Government to use the invention in question, it may order revocation of the patent.

206. The court may also revoke a patent which has already expired.

289. Aloys Wobber & Anr. v. Yogesh Mehra & Ors. AIR 2014 SC 2210.
290. Ajay Industrial Corporation v. Shiro Kanao, AIR 1983 Del 496.
291. Shamnad Basheer v. Union Of India W.P.(C) 5590/2015.

§3. SURRENDER OF PATENTS

207. A patentee may, at any time, offer to surrender his/her patent by giving notice in the prescribed manner to the Controller.[292]

208. Section 63 read with Rule 87 sets out the procedure for advertising the offer of surrender and inviting notice of opposition. This procedure must be followed to protect the interests of licensees, equitable assignees and others with whom the patentee might have contractual obligations that are dependent upon the continuance of the patent.

292. Section 63(1).

Chapter 9. Infringement and Remedies

209. Infringement: The Act does not define what constitutes infringement of a patent. It has to be deduced from the scope of the monopoly rights conferred on the patentee. In other words, it may be said that infringement is the violation of those monopoly rights.

210. The patentee, his/her agents and licensees have the exclusive right under section 48 to make, use, exercise, sell or distribute the patented invention in India. Therefore, to decide whether an act amounts to infringement, the following aspects may be examined: the extent of monopoly rights granted to the patentee, his/her agents and licensees and the acts of the alleged infringer and whether they amount to making, using, exercising, selling or distributing a product.[293]

211. The onus of proof of establishing infringement is on the plaintiff, as it is the plaintiff who alleges that the defendant has infringed his/her patent. However, this general principle based on the laws of evidence may, in certain cases of process patents, shift the onus onto the defendant.[294] This court may pass such an order for shift in the burden of proof in two scenarios:

(1) The subject matter of the patent is a process for obtaining a new product; and
(2) There is a substantial likelihood that the identical product is made by the process, and the patentee or a person deriving title or interest in the patent from him has been unable through reasonable efforts to determine the process actually used.

212. The patentee is, however, under no obligation to give notice to the infringer about the fact that the latter is infringing the rights of the patentee as a pre-condition to bringing action against the infringer. However, the patentee's conduct should not amount to acquiescence. If acquiescence on the part of the patentee is proved, the court will not allow the plea of infringement. It may be noted that as far as infringement is concerned, intention to infringe, or the absence of such intention, is not to be taken into account.[295]

213. Under the provisions of section 105, a person may obtain a declaration from the court to the effect that the use by him/her of any process or the making, use or sale of the article does not constitute an infringement of a patent claim, even though no assertion to the contrary has been made by the patentee or the licensee. To obtain such a declaration, it must be shown that the person seeking the declaration had applied to the patentee or exclusive licensee for a written acknowledgement of non-infringement and had furnished full particulars in writing of the process or article in question and that the patentee or licensee had refused or neglected to

293. Dudgeon v. Thomson (1877) 3 App Cas 34, F. Hoffman-La Roche Ltd. & Anr. v. Cipla Ltd. (2012) 52 PTC 1 (Del).
294. Section 104A, Farbewerke Hoechst v. Unichem Laboratories and Ors. AIR 1969 Bom 255.
295. Tweedle v. Ashworth, 7 RPC 426.

give such an acknowledgement. The validity of a claim of the specification of a patent shall not be called into question in a suit for a declaration under section 105. Accordingly, the making or refusal of such a declaration in the case of a patent shall not be deemed to imply that the patent is valid or invalid.[296]

Section 106 grants power to the court to provide relief in cases of groundless threats of infringement proceedings.[297] Section 107 states that in any suit for infringement, all grounds of revocation under section 64 are available as grounds for defence.[298]

No suit for a declaration under section 105 or for any relief under section 106 or for infringement of a patent shall be instituted in any court inferior to a district court having jurisdiction to try the suit. In case a counterclaim for revocation is filed by the defendant, the suit, along with the counterclaim, will be transferred to the High Court for decision.[299]

Section 107A provides for exemptions from infringement claims in certain cases, i.e., any act of making, constructing, using, selling or importing a patented invention solely for uses reasonably related to the development and submission of information required under any law for the time being in force, in India, or in another country, that regulates the manufacture, construction, use, sale of import of any product. It further includes importation of patented products by any person from a person who is duly authorized under the law to produce and sell or distribute the product, which shall not be considered as an infringement of patent rights.[300] The expanse of this provision has been extended to include exports as per the Delhi High Court judgment in the case of *Bayer Corporation v. Natco.*[301] The presiding judge on this matter, Justice Endlaw, held that the export of a patented invention for the purpose of experimentation would be covered within the confines of section 107 of the Patents Act, 1970, and thus not amount to cause an infringement. As a result, Natco was allowed to export Bayer's patented drug 'Sorafenib Tosylate' (for which it was granted a compulsory licence in 2012) to China for the purpose of conducting development/clinical studies and trials. On appeal, the Division Bench of the Delhi High Court reaffirmed the Single Judge's decision.[302]

214. Remedies: The remedies that are available to the aggrieved party in a suit for infringement of patent rights include:[303]

- injunction; and
- damages or account of profits (at the option of the plaintiff).

---

296. Section 105(1)(b).
297. S. Ram Kumar v. Micromax Informatics Limited (2010) 44 PTC 409 (P&H).
298. Fabcon v. Industrial Engineering Corporation, AIR 1987 All 338, Cadila Pharmaceuticals Ltd. v. Instacare Laboratories (2001) PTC 472 (Guj).
299. Section 104, FDC Limited & Ors. v. Sanjeev Khandelwal (2007) 35 PTC 436 (Mad), LG Electronics India Pvt. Ltd. v. Bharat Bhogilal Patel (2012) 51 PTC 513 (Del).
300. Section 107A.
301. Bayer Corporation v. Natco W.P.(C) 1971/2014.
302. Bayer Corporation v. Union Of India & Ors. LPA No. 359/2017.
303. Section 108.

215. Under section 108, the granting of these remedies is discretionary. Section 108 is not exhaustive on the kinds of reliefs that may be granted, and the courts are not debarred from ordering delivery up or destruction of the infringing articles.

216. Injunctions: An injunction is a preventive relief. It may be made subject to such conditions, as the court may think fit to impose. In all cases, an injunction will be limited to the term of the patent. Injunctions may be temporary or permanent. However, in a suit for infringement of a patent, there can be no perpetual injunction as the injunction will be limited to the term of the patent. Where there are a number of patents involved in an infringement, and this usually happens in the case of process patents, and the plaintiff could not specify which of them has been infringed, injunction may be limited to the oldest of the unexpired patents, that is, the patent which expires first. An interlocutory injunction may also be granted by the courts to restrain the defendant from committing the acts complained of till further or final order is made. Interlocutory injunction may be granted restraining the defendant from parting with possession, custody or control of the infringing goods without the consent of the plaintiff.[304] The object of the interlocutory injunction is to protect the plaintiff against injury by violation of his or her rights for which he/she could not be adequately compensated in damages if the trial goes in his/her favour.[305] In cases of interlocutory injunction, including any patent action, the principle is the same. The plaintiff must prove/show prima facie case that the patent is valid and infringed; balance of convenience is in favour of plaintiff; and irreparable loss that may be caused to the plaintiff by not granting an order of injunction.[306]

217. An ex parte injunction was allowed in a case where a certificate of validity of a patent was granted in a proceeding, and a temporary injunction for a short period was granted by the Court of Appeal to give the plaintiff an opportunity of applying to the trial judge to hear the case.[307] Interlocutory injunction has been granted on an ex parte motion where a prima facie case of infringement was established.[308]

218. The enforcement of an injunction is by way of committal to civil prison or by attachment of the property of the defendant.[309]

219. Damages or Account of Profits: When interlocutory injunction has been refused, the court may order the defendants to maintain correct and regular accounts

304. Hoovercraft Development Ltd v. Sealand Hoovercoraft Ltd (1976) RPC 393.
305. Wockhardt Limited v. Hetero Drugs Ltd. & Others (2006) 32 PTC 65 (Mad).
306. Bajaj Auto Ltd. v. TVS Motor Company Ltd.
307. British Thomson-Houston Co Ltd v. Phillip Henry & Co Ltd 45 RPC 218; FDC Limited & Ors. v. Sanjeev Khandelwal & Ors. (2007) 35 PTC 436 (Mad); Morgan Stanley Mutual Fund v. Kartick Das (1994) 4 SCC 225.
308. Hoffman-La Roche & Co AG v. Curtis & Co Ltd (1968) RPC 87.
309. Order 21, Rule 32(1) of Code of Civil Procedure, 1908.

of their business in respect of the alleged use of the patented invention and file a copy of the accounts periodically in the court, with a copy to the plaintiff.[310]

220. The court may grant either damages or an account of profits. However, where the defendant proves that at the time of the infringement he/she was not aware and had no reasonable grounds to believe that the patent existed, damages or account of profits will not be granted.[311]

221. In assessing damages, the only question to be asked is what is the loss sustained by the patentee by reason of the unlawful sale of the defendant's goods. The loss must be the natural and direct consequence of the defendant's acts.[312] It is unreasonable to give the patentee profits, which were not earned by the use of his or her invention.[313]

222. Delivery Up or Destruction: It is in the discretion of the court to make an order for delivering up or destroying the infringing articles. Such an order is not meant to be a punishment to the infringer, but rather to give relief to the patentee by preventing the defendant from making use of the infringing articles which might be in his/her possession.[314] Where the defendants gave an undertaking to deliver up the drawings to the plaintiff, and the plaintiff gave an undertaking to take no further step in the action, it was ordered that the defendants should file an affidavit accounting for all copies of the drawings that had been in their possession and power.[315]

223. Other offences and penalties under the Act are as follows:

- Section 118 deals with contravention of secrecy provisions in a case where the patent relates to an invention relevant for defence purposes. The Controller may give directions prohibiting or restricting the publication or communication of information relating to such invention. Any person who fails to comply with any such direction will be punishable with imprisonment for a maximum term of two years, or with a fine, or with both.
- Section 122 deals with the failure to supply certain information where the Central Government authorizes the use of an invention by any Government undertaking; the Controller may, during the continuance of a patent, require a patentee or a licensee to furnish periodical statements. In addition, all patentees and licensees are required to furnish periodical statements about the commercial working of the patent to the Controller.[316] Any person who fails to comply with these requirements will be punishable with a fine, which may extend to Indian Rupee (INR) 10 lakh.

310. Ram Narain Kher v. Ambassador Industries AIR 1976 Del 87 at 90; Microsoft Corporation v. K. Mayuri (2007) 35 PTC 415 (Del).
311. Section 111(1).
312. United Horse Shoe & Nail Co Ltd v. Stewart & Co 5 RPC 260.
313. Ibid.
314. Farbewerke Hoechst v. Unichem Laboratories And Ors. AIR 1969 Bom 255.
315. Kangol Industries Ltd v. Alfred Bray & Sons Ltd 70 RPC 15.
316. Section 146(2).

- Section 119 deals with falsification of entries in the register kept under the Act. If any person makes or causes to be made any false entry in the register, such person will be punishable with imprisonment for a term up to two years, or with a fine, or with both.
- Section 121 states that the wrongful use of the words 'patent office' in a place of business or in any document or in any other manner that would reasonably lead to the belief that such place of business is officially connected with the Patent Office will be punishable with imprisonment up to six months, or with a fine, or with both.
- Section 120 deals with the unauthorized claim of patent rights and the making of false representations by a person that any article sold by him/her is patented in India or is the subject of an application for a patent in India and states that such acts are punishable with a fine, which may extend to INR 1 lakh.
- Section 123 deals with the practice as patent agent by a non-registered patent agent and states that a person cannot describe or hold him/herself out as a patent agent unless he/she is registered as such under the Act. Contravention of this provision is punishable with a fine extending up to INR 1 lakh in the case of a first offence and INR 5 lakhs in the case of subsequent offences.
- Section 124 deals with offences by companies, wherein the company as well as every person in charge of or responsible to the company for its business at the time of the offence shall be deemed to be guilty of the offence and shall be liable to be punished accordingly. However, if such person proves that the offence was committed without his or her knowledge or that he/she exercised all due diligence to prevent the commission of such offence, he or she shall not be punished.

Chapter 10. Patent (Amendment) Rules, 2024

224. The Indian Patent Office published the Patent (Amendment) Rules, 2024, on its official website on 16 March 2024 and eventually came into effect on 15 March 2024.

225. Several important and significant changes have been introduced in the said Amendment. The following outlines the significant changes that have been brought around by the said amendment:

> Amendment of Rule 12: Applicants will no longer be required to submit Form 3 on multiple instances. With the amendment to sub-rule 2 of rule 12, Applicants will now have to submit the detailed particulars of any corresponding foreign application through Form 3 within three months from the date of issuance of the first statements of objections under sub-rule (3) of rule 24B or sub-rule (8) of rule 24C.

226. The burden of submitting information relating to objections, if any, in respect of novelty and patentability of the invention and any other particulars which may include claims of application allowed has been relaxed. The controller may use accessible and available databases, for considering the information relating to applications filed in a country outside India without having to rely on the Applicant to submit these details.

227. Two new sub-rules have been inserted. Sub-rule 4 will now allow the controller to direct the applicant to furnish a fresh statement and undertaking in Form 3 within two months of the date of such communication by the Controller with reasons recorded in writing.

228. Sub-rule 5 seeks to allow the controller to condone the delay or extend the time for filing Form 3 for a period of up to three months upon a request made in Form 4.

229. Change to Rule 13: Under Rule 13, sub-rule 2A has been inserted which provides clarity on the content of divisional applications. As per the new sub-rule, a patent applicant files one or more further divisional applications under section 16, in respect of an invention disclosed in either a provisional or complete specification or a further application filed under section 16.

230. Change to Rule 24B: Examination of Application – The timeline to file a request for examination has now been reduced to thirty-one months. A request for examination will now have to be made within thirty-one months. A request for examination will now have to be made within thirty-one months from the date of filing the application or the date of priority, whichever is earlier. In the case of divisional applications, a request for examination will have to be filed within thirty-one months from the date of filing of the main / parent application or within six months from the date of filing the divisional application.

231. A new Rule 29A has been inserted which introduces a new Form called Form 31 to be used for availing the grace period specified under section 31.

232. In case of pre-grant representations, the controller will now be required to check if a prima facie case has been made out in the pre-grant representation and whether the Opponent has requested for any opportunity to be heard.

233. Two new additional sub-rules 5A and 5B have been inserted which read as follows:

> (5A.) The Procedure specified in sub-rules (2) to (4) of rule 62 shall, as far as may be, apply to the procedure for hearing under this rule.
> (5B) An application for a patent, in which a representation for opposition.

234. Under the amendments carried out to sub-rule 4 of Rule 56, the Opposition Board will now have to conduct an examination of the notice of opposition along with documents filed under Rules 57 to 60 and submit a report with reasons on each ground taken in the notice of opposition with its joint recommendation within two months from the date on which the documents were forwarded to them.

235. A new Rule 70A has been introduced which will allow the controller to issue a certificate of inventorship to an inventor in respect of a patent in force. Such a request will have to be made by the inventor through a new form called Form 8A. Duplicate certificate of inventorship may also be requested in case the original certificate of inventorship is lost, destroyed, damaged or cannot be produced.

236. Change to Rule 80: In case a Patentee chooses to pay renewal fees in advance for at least four years, the patentee can obtain a 10% reduction fees, provided the fees are paid electronically.

237. Change under Rule 137: The same provides the controller the power to extend time under Rule 12(5), that is, delayed submission of statements and undertakings regarding foreign applications, the time limit to enter the national phase under Rule 20(4), and the time limit to file the English translation of the description, claims, drawings and abstract that form part of the PCT Application under Rule 20(6).

238. The timeline pertaining to submission of priority documents and English translation of the priority documents under Rule 21.

239. The deadline to file a reply to the first statement of objections (FER Response) and the extension of the time available under Rules 24B(5) and 24B(6), respectively.

240. The deadline to file a response to the FER and the extension of time available in case of expedited examinations under Rules 24C(10) and 24C(11), respectively.

Part III. Trademarks

Chapter 1. Sources and Legislation

241. The law governing trademarks and trade names was the Trade and Merchandise Marks Act of 1958 (Act of 1958), along with the Trade and Merchandise Marks Rules of 1959. Under the TRIPS Agreement, India was required to amend its laws relating to Trademarks and Geographical Indications of Goods.

242. Major changes have been made in the laws relating to trademarks to ensure compliance with TRIPS. The Trademarks Act, 1999 (Act of 1999), has now replaced the four-decade-old Trade and Merchandise Marks Act of 1958 and is intended to provide for registration and better protection of trademarks for goods and services and for the prevention of the use of fraudulent marks. The Act came into force on 15 September 2003. Two new chapters have been added to the Act of 1999, one dealing with 'Collective Marks' (Chapter VIII) and the other with 'Appellate Board' (Chapter XI).

243. Chapter VIII dealing with 'Collective Marks' lays down special provisions for application, registration, infringement and removal of registration of collective marks. Chapter XI, which deals with 'Appellate Board', provides for the establishment and composition of the Appellate Board, the qualifications, term and powers of the members of the board, appeals to the board and the procedure thereof and other such related matters.

244. The Trade Marks Act, 1999, was amended in 2010, vide the Trade Marks (Amendment) Act, 2010, which came into force on 8 July 2013.

Chapter 2. Subject Matter of Protection

§1. Signs Which May Serve as Trademarks

245. The Trademark Act of 1999 defines 'mark' as per section 2(1)(m) as any device, brand, heading, label, ticket, name, signature, word, letter, numeral, shape of goods, packaging or combination of colours or any combination thereof. This is a more exhaustive definition as compared with the 1958 Act, which did not cover shape of goods, packaging or combination of colours. It is an inclusive one and may include other things also. Thus, the definition of trademark is very wide and refers to a mark capable of being represented graphically and which is capable of distinguishing the goods or services of one person from those of others.[317]

Section 9 lays down the grounds on which a trademark may be refused registration. In addition, section 10 (Limitation as to colour), section 11 (Relative grounds for refusal of registration), section 12 (Registration in case of honest concurrent use), section 13 (Prohibition of registration of certain names as trademarks), section 14 (Use of names and representations of living persons or persons recently dead), sections 15 and 16 (Registration of trademarks as a series or as associated trademarks) state in detail the other requisites for registration of trademarks.

§2. Absolute and Relative Grounds for Refusal of Registration

246. Section 9(1) lists the grounds for refusal of registration of a trademark. Registration may be denied if such trademarks:

- are devoid of any distinctive character;
- are not capable of distinguishing the goods or services of one person from those of another;
- consist exclusively of marks which are used in the trade to designate the kind, quality, quantity, intended purpose, values, geographical origin or the time of production of the goods or rendering of services or which represent other characteristics of the goods or services; or
- consist exclusively of marks which have become customary in the current language or in the bona fide or established practices of the trade.[318]

However, a trademark shall not be refused registration if it has acquired a distinctive character as a result of the use made of it before the date of application or if it is already a well-known trademark. The Supreme Court has held that '*a descriptive trademark may be entitled to protection, if it has assumed a secondary meaning which identifies it with a particular product or as being from a particular*

317. Laxmikant V. Patel v. Chetanbhat Shah, AIR 2002 SC 275.
318. Himalaya Drug Company v. S.B.L. Limited (2013) 53 PTC 1 (Del); Orchid Chemicals & Pharmaceuticals Ltd. v. Wockhardt Ltd. (2013) 56 PTC 558 (Mad).

source'.[319] Also, a descriptive mark cannot be registered, i.e., if it imparts information directly. A descriptive mark is a word, picture or other symbol that directly describes something about the goods or services in connection with which it was used as a mark.[320] For instance, the words 'tastee' and 'sugar free' were found to be descriptive and generic as marks, respectively.[321]

247. According to section 9(2), a mark shall also not be registered as a trademark if:

- it is of such nature as to deceive the public or cause confusion;[322]
- it contains or comprises any matter likely to hurt the religious susceptibilities of any class or sections of citizens of India;
- it comprises or contains scandalous or obscene matter;
- its use is prohibited under the Emblems and Names (Prevention of Improper Use) Act, 1950.

248. Section 9(3) states that a mark shall also not be registered as a trademark if it consists exclusively of:

- the shape of goods which result from the nature of goods themselves; or
- a shape of goods which is necessary to obtain a technical result; or
- the shape which gives substantial value to the goods.

However, for the purposes of section 9, the nature of goods or services in relation to which the trademark is used or is proposed to be used shall not be a ground for refusal of registration.

249. Section 11 of the 1999 Act lays down the relative grounds for refusal of registration of a trademark. It states that a mark shall not be registered:

(1) if there is likelihood of confusion caused to the public by virtue of its identity with an earlier trademark providing similar goods or services or its similarity with an earlier trademark providing identical goods or services;[323]

---

319. Godfrey Philips India Ltd. v. Girnar Food & Beverages Ltd. (2004) 5 SCC 257; see also Bharatbhai Khushalbhai Patel v. Deluxe Limited & Ors. (2013) 56 PTC 451 (Guj); Pidilite Industries v. Jubiliant Agri & Consumer Products Limited (2014) 57 PTC 617 (Bom); IHHR Hospitality v. Bestech India Pvt. Ltd. (2012) 50 PTC 535.
320. Consim Info Pvt. Ltd. v. Google India Pvt. Ltd. (2013) 54 PTC 578 (Mad).
321. Marico Ltd. v. Agro Tech Foods Ltd. (2010) 44 PTC 736 (Del); Eatman Foods India Pvt. Ltd. v. Savorit Ltd. (2013) 56 PTC 576.
322. Parker Knoll Ltd. v. Knoll International Ltd. 1962 RPC 265; Amritdhara Pharmacy v. Satya Deo Gupta (1963) 2 SCR 484.
323. National Sewing Thread Co. v. James Chadwick, AIR 1953 SC 357, BDH Industries v. Croydon Chemical Works Ltd., AIR 2002 Bom 361.

(2) as per Clause (2) if it is identical or similar to an earlier trademark and is to be registered for goods or services which are not similar to those provided by the earlier trademark;[324]

(3) as per Clause (3) if its use in India is liable to be prevented under the law relating to passing off protecting an unregistered mark or if the use of such a mark is prevented by virtue of law of copyright.

250. The 1999 Act has done away with the concept of dividing the Register of Trademarks into Parts A and B. Therefore, there is now only one consolidated Register in which all registered trademarks are entered. Accordingly, section 6(7) of the Act of 1999 states that the Register of Trademarks, which includes both Part A and Part B, existing at the commencement of the Act of 1999, shall be incorporated in and form part of the register under the Act of 1999.

324. Rolex SA v. Alex Jewellery Pvt. Ltd (2009) 41 PTC 284 (Del), Tata Sons Ltd. v. Tata Industrial Recruitment (2009) 41 PTC 753 (Del), Bharti Airtel v. Rajeev Kumar (2013) 53 PTC 568 (Del).

Chapter 3. Formalities

251. Section 18 sets out the procedure to be followed by an applicant for registration of his/her trademark. Any person claiming to be the proprietor of a trademark used or proposed to be used by him/her, and who is desirous of registering it, shall apply in writing to the Registrar in the prescribed manner for the registration of his/her trademark. An application shall not be made in respect of goods or services comprised of more than one prescribed class of goods. A person who does not use or propose to use a mark is not entitled to make an application for registration of a mark.

252. Every application shall be filed in the office of the Trademarks Registry within whose territorial limits the first-mentioned applicant's principal place of business in India is situated, provided where the applicant or any of the joint applicants does not carry on business in India, the application shall be filed in the office of the Trademarks Registry within whose territorial limits the address for service in India is situated.

253. Under sections 18(4) and (5), the Registrar may refuse the application or may accept it absolutely or subject to such amendments, modifications, conditions or limitations, if any, as he/she may think fit. In the case of a refusal or conditional acceptance of an application, the Registrar shall record in writing the grounds for such refusal or conditional acceptance and the material used by him/her in arriving at his/her decision.

254. When an application for registration is made, it is first examined in the Trademarks Registry to see whether the formalities have been observed. For deciding the rights of an applicant, the register and pending applications are searched in order to find out whether any other identical or similar mark has already been registered, or registration has been sought in respect of the same or similar description of goods. Where a similar mark has already been registered, all particulars with regard to the registered mark will be given to the applicant, and that mark will be made a ground of objection to his/her application under section 12. If there are pending applications that conflict, then the Registrar will notify all the applicants of the conflicting marks.

255. The onus of proving that a mark is entitled to be registered is on the applicant.[325] It is for the applicant to satisfy the Registrar that the trademark which he/she seeks to register is not likely to deceive or to cause confusion, and that it does not fall within the prohibition of section 11 of the Act of 1958.[326] Where the mark is

325. Notos Ltd's Application (1931) 48 RPC 168, 177: James Chadwick & Bros Ltd v. The National Sewing Thread Co Ltd (1951) 54 Bom LR 556, 568: Re National Sewing Thread Co Ltd's Application AIR 1953 SC 357, 363; Prem Nath v. Registrar AIR 1972 Cal 261, 264.

326. National Sewing Thread Co Ltd v. James Chadwick & Bros Ltd AIR 1953 SC 357; Prem Nath Mayer v. Registrar of Trademarks AIR 1972 Cal 261; Dyer Meakin Breweries v. Scotch Whisky Association AIR 1980 Del 125, 128.

prima facie not distinctive, the applicant should produce evidence by way of affidavit,[327] to prove that the mark has become distinctive by use. The Supreme Court observed in the case of *Khoday India Ltd v. The Scotch Whisky Association*[328] that the test of deceptive similarity applicable in each case should differ depending on the nature and kind of customers who would like to buy the goods and when and how they are likely to be deceived.

256. Under section 22, it is expressly provided that the Registrar may at any time, whether before or after acceptance of the application, permit correction of any error in, or in connection with, the application or permit an amendment of the application or permit the correction of any error in, or an amendment of, a notice of opposition or a counterstatement made under section 21 of the 1999 Act. Where an amendment would entirely alter the nature of the application and the nature of the opposition proceedings, the Registrar must necessarily refuse the application. In any case, even after amendment, an opportunity must be given to the other side to lead, if necessary, any evidence and make his/her submissions.[329]

257. Where a trademark contains a word or words in characters other than Devanagri or Roman, that shall, unless the Registrar otherwise directs, be endorsed on the application form and copies thereof and on each of the accompanying representations, a transliteration and translation to the satisfaction of the Registrar, of each of such words, and every such endorsement shall state the language to which the word belongs and shall be signed by the applicant (Rule 33 of the Trade Marks Rules, 2002).

258. Where an applicant dies after the date of application, but before registration, the Registrar will allow the application to be amended so that the name of his/her successor in interest may appear in the place of the applicant. However, in such a case, it will be necessary to produce before the Registrar proof of the applicant's death and proof of transmission of the interest of the deceased person to the claiming successor (Rule 61 of the Trade Marks Rules, 2002).

259. According to section 19 of the 1999 Act, where after the acceptance of an application for registration of a trademark, but before its registration, the Registrar is satisfied that the application has been accepted in error or that in the circumstances of the case the trademark should not be registered or should be registered subject to conditions or limitations or to conditions additional to or different from the conditions or limitations subject to which the application has been accepted, the Registrar may, after hearing the applicant, if he/she so desires, withdraw the acceptance and proceed as if the application had not been accepted. The procedure to be followed in case of withdrawal of acceptance by the Registrar is set out in Rule 42.

327. See s. 99.
328. AIR 2008 SC 2737.
329. The Scientific Soap Works v. D.M. Shah (1957) Bom 564: 59 Bom LR 539; AIR 1958 Bom 47; American Home Products Corp v. Mac Laboratories (1986) 1 SCC 465; Whirlpool Corporation v. Registrar of Trade Marks (1998) 8 SCC 1.

260. Even though the Registrar may have accepted an application, the Central Government[330] may direct the Registrar to refuse registration of a mark. In such a case, the applicant would have no right of appeal. Moreover, before the registration is granted, the applicant has no right to assert that the trademark has been infringed.[331]

261. Section 20 states that when an application for registration of a trademark has been accepted, whether absolutely or subject to conditions or limitations, the Registrar shall cause the application to be advertised in the prescribed manner. It is also provided that the Registrar may cause the application to be advertised before acceptance, where it appears to him/her that it is expedient by reason of any exceptional circumstances to do so.

262. Anyone who wishes to oppose the mark must do so within four months of its advertisement. The grounds of opposition should be stated in the notice with the particulars of the advertisement in the prescribed journal and the class of goods under which the mark is advertised (Rule 47). Within two months from receipt of the notice of opposition, the applicant has to file a counterstatement in duplicate, in Form TM-5, in which he/she should set out his/her answer to the notice of opposition (Rule 49). The opponent, on receipt of the counterstatement, should, within two months, provide evidence in support of the grounds of opposition by way of affidavit, or intimate to the Registrar and to the applicant that he/she does not desire to adduce evidence in support of his/her opposition, but intends to rely on the facts stated in the notice of opposition (Rule 50(1)). If he/she does not do so, he/she shall be deemed to have abandoned his/her opposition (Rule 50(2)). However, if the opponent does produce evidence in support of the opposition, the applicant should leave with the Registrar such evidence, by way of affidavit, as he/she desires to adduce in support of his/her application, within two months from receipt of the opponent's affidavit (Rule 51). Within one month from the receipt of the applicant's affidavits, the opponent should leave evidence, by way of reply, with the Registrar (Rule 52). The case is then ready for hearing, and a date is fixed by the Registrar for hearing the opposition proceedings (Rule 56). The Registrar has the discretionary power to grant an additional month for making submissions under Rules 50 and 51 above.

263. After hearing the parties, the Registrar shall give his/her decision in writing and send the same to the applicant and the opponent or opponents. If the opposition is dismissed, then subject to appeal from the decision of the Registrar to the High Court, the procedure for registering the trademark is duly gone through.

264. Under section 22 of the 1999 Act, it is expressly provided that the Registrar may at any time, whether before or after acceptance of the application, permit correction of any error in or in connection with the application, or permit an amendment of the application. Where an amendment would entirely alter the nature of the

330. The Central Government is empowered to issue directions under s. 23(1).
331. K.R. Narayanan and Anr v. S. Murali (AIR 2008 SC 3216).

application and the nature of the opposition proceedings, the Registrar must necessarily refuse the application. In any case, even after amendment, an opportunity must be given to the other side to lead, if necessary, any evidence and make his/her submissions.

265. Section 23 provides for the registration of trademarks. When an application for registration of a trademark has been accepted, and either the application has not been opposed and the time for notice of opposition has expired, or the application has been opposed and the opposition has been decided in favour of the applicant, the Registrar shall, unless the Central Government otherwise directs, register the said trademark within eighteen months of the filing of the application. The trademark when registered shall be registered as of the date of making of the said application. Therefore, a suit for infringement of trademark filed during the pendency of an application for registration would be competent in cases where the trademark is registered on acceptance of such application.[332]

On the registration of a trademark, the Registrar shall issue the applicant a certificate, in the prescribed form, of the registration thereof, sealed with the seal of the Trademarks Registry. Once the registration of the mark is granted to the registered proprietor, it is deemed to be publicly used from the date of the application for registration.[333]

266. According to section 23(3), where the registration of a trademark is not completed within twelve months from the date of the application, by reason of default on the part of the applicant, the Registrar may, after giving notice to the applicant in the prescribed manner, treat the application as abandoned unless it is completed within the time specified in that behalf in the notice.

332. P.L. Anwar Basha v. M. Natarajan AIR 1980 Mad 56. The plaint was amended after registration, and the prayer against infringement was added.
333. Wockhardt Ltd. v. Eden Healthcare (2014) 58 PTC 14 (Bom).

Chapter 4. Ownership and Transfer

267. According to section 38, a registered trademark is assignable and transmissible. It states that, notwithstanding anything to the contrary in any other law, a registered trademark shall, subject to other provisions of this Act, be assignable and transmissible, whether with or without the goodwill of the business concerned and in respect of either all or some of the goods or services in respect of which the trademark is registered.

268. Section 37 sets out provisions that empower a registered proprietor to assign a trademark and give receipts for the consideration received. On such assignment, the original proprietor loses all rights over the trademark and they become vested in the assignee.[334]

269. Section 39 deals with the assignability and transmissibility of unregistered trademarks. It states that an unregistered trademark may be assigned or transmitted with or without the goodwill of the business concerned.

270. Section 40 places certain restrictions on the assignment or transmission of a trademark where multiple exclusive rights would be created. It states that notwithstanding the provisions of sections 37 and 38 of the Act of 1999, a trademark shall not be assignable or transmissible where, as a result of the assignment or transmission, there would subsist, whether under this Act or any other law, exclusive rights in more than one of the persons concerned to the use, in relation to the same goods or description of goods, of trademarks nearly resembling each other or of identical trademarks, if, having regard to the similarity of the goods and of the trademarks, the use of the trademarks in exercise of those rights would be likely to deceive or cause confusion.

271. However, the proviso to the section states that an assignment or transmission shall not be deemed to be invalid if the exclusive rights subsisting are, having regard to limitations imposed thereon, such as not to be exercisable by two or more of those persons in relation to goods to be sold or otherwise traded in, within India otherwise than for export there from, or in relation to goods to be exported to the same market outside India.

272. The proprietor of a registered trademark who proposes to assign it may submit a statement of the case in the prescribed manner to the Registrar setting out the circumstances, and the Registrar may issue him/her a certificate stating whether, having regard to the similarity of the goods and of the trademarks referred to in the case, the proposed assignment would or would not be invalid. A certificate so issued shall, subject to appeal and unless it is shown that the certificate was obtained by fraud or misrepresentation, be conclusive evidence as to the validity or invalidity of the assignment in so far as validity or invalidity depends upon the facts set out in

334. B.D.A. Ltd v. State of Uttar Pradesh AIR 1995 All 277; see also Wonderworld Electrodes etc. v. Ahura Welding etc., 2003 (26) PTC 37 (Mad).

the case, but, as regards a certificate in favour of validity, only if application under section 45 for the registration of the title of the person becoming entitled is made within six months from the date on which the certificate is issued.[335]

273. Section 41 also places certain restrictions on the assignment or transmission of a trademark when exclusive rights would be created in different parts of India. It states that, notwithstanding the provisions of section 38 and section 39, a trademark shall not be assignable or transmissible in a case in which as a result of the assignment or transmission there would subsist, whether under this Act or any other law, an exclusive right in one of the persons concerned to the use of the trademark limited to use in relation to goods to be sold, or otherwise traded in, in any place in India, and an exclusive right in another of these persons to the use of a trademark nearly resembling the first-mentioned trademark or of an identical trademark in relation to the same goods or description of goods limited to use in relation to goods to be sold, or otherwise traded in, in any other place in India.

274. However, the proviso to the section states that on the application by the proprietor of a trademark who proposes to assign it, or by a person who claims that a registered trademark has been transmitted to him/her, the Registrar, if he/she is satisfied that the use of the trademark in exercise of the said right would not be contrary to the public interest, may approve the assignment or transmission. Such an assignment or transmission when approved shall, unless it is shown that the approval was obtained by fraud or misrepresentation, be deemed to be valid under this section. This is only if application for the registration, under section 45, of the title of the person becoming entitled is made within six months from the date on which the approval is given or, in the case of a transmission, was made before that date.

275. Section 42 lays down conditions for assignment of a trademark otherwise than in connection with the goodwill of a business. It provides that where an assignment of a trademark, whether registered or unregistered, is made otherwise than in connection with the goodwill of the business, the assignment shall not take effect unless the assignee, not later than the expiration of six months from the date on which the assignment is made or within such extended period as the Registrar may allow, applies to the Registrar for directions with respect to the advertisement of the assignment, and advertises it in such form and manner and within such period as the Registrar may direct.

276. However, an assignment of a trademark in the following manner shall not be deemed to be an assignment made otherwise than in connection with the goodwill of the business:

– an assignment of a trademark in respect only of some of the goods or services for which the trademark is registered, accompanied by the transfer of the goodwill of the business concerned in those goods only; or

335. Section 41(2).

- an assignment of a trademark used in relation to goods exported from India, or in relation to services for use outside India, if the assignment is accompanied by the transfer of the goodwill of the export business only.

As per the provisions of section 43, a certification trademark shall not be assignable or transmissible otherwise than with the consent of the Registrar, for which application shall be made in writing in the prescribed manner.

277. Provisions for the registration of assignments and transmissions are set out in section 45. It states that a person entitled by assignment or transmission to a registered trademark shall apply to the Registrar to register his/her title. The particulars of the assignment or transmission shall also be entered on the register. However, where the validity of an assignment or transmission is in dispute between the parties, the Registrar may refuse to register the assignment or transmission until the rights of the parties have been determined by a competent court. A document or instrument, in respect of which no entry has been made in the register, shall not be admitted in evidence by the Registrar or the Appellate Board or any court, in proof of title to the trademark by assignment or transmission, unless the Registrar or the court directs otherwise.[336]

336. Cinni Foundation v. Raj Kumar Sah (2009) 41 PTC 320 (Del); Skol Breweries v. Som Distilleries (2010) 42 PTC 389 (Bom).

Chapter 5. Scope of Exclusive Rights

278. Section 28 sets out the exclusive rights of the proprietor of a registered trademark under the Act. It states that the registered proprietor of a trademark shall have the exclusive right to use the mark in relation to the goods or services in respect of which it is registered and will be entitled to obtain relief where there is an infringement of this right. This right will be subject to the conditions and limitations under which the registration was obtained. An exception to this exclusive right is in a case where two or more persons are registered proprietors of trademarks that are identical with or nearly resemble each other. In such a situation, neither of the registered proprietors will be deemed to have an exclusive right over their marks as against each other but will have the same rights as other registered proprietors as against all other parties.

279. In all legal proceedings relating to a registered trademark, as per the provisions of section 31, the original registration of the mark and all subsequent assignments and transmissions thereof shall be prima facie evidence of the validity of such registered trademark, until the mark is deleted or expunged from the register.[337]

280. Section 32 states that where a trademark is registered in breach of section 9(1), it shall not be declared invalid if, in consequence of the use which has been made of it, it has, after registration and before commencement of any legal proceedings challenging the validity of such registration, acquired a distinctive character in relation to the goods or services for which it is registered.[338] Section 33 deals with the effect of acquiescence by the proprietor of an earlier trademark to the use of a registered mark for a continuous period of five years.

337. P.M. Diesels Pvt Ltd v. Thukral Mechanical Works AIR 1988 Del 282; Rana Steels v. Ran India Steels Ltd. (2008) 37 PTC 24 (Del); Wyeth Holdings Corporation v. Burnet Pharmaceuticals (2008) 36 PTC 478 (Bom).
338. Consim Info Pvt. Ltd. v. Google India Pvt. Ltd. (2013) 54 PTC 578 (Mad).

Chapter 6. Limitation of the Scope of Trademark Protection

281. 'Limitations', as defined in section 2(1)(l), means any limitations of the exclusive right to the use of a trademark, given by the registration of a person as proprietor thereof, including limitations of that right as to mode or area within India, or outside India. Limitations as to the use of a trademark are of various kinds, and a trademark may be registered with territorial, colour, mode of use and other such restrictions.

282. The following are some examples of restrictions imposed on the use of trademarks:

- the mark shall not be used as a back stamp;
- the mark shall not be affixed to goods by way of adhesive printed label and that it shall be marked upon the goods by means of a metal dye;
- the mark shall be used only as a selvedge stamp;
- the blank spaces in the mark shall, when the mark is in use, be occupied only by matter of a wholly descriptive and non-trademark character.

283. Furthermore, according to section 27, no person shall be entitled to institute any proceeding to prevent, or recover damages for, the infringement of an unregistered trademark. Thus, only a registered proprietor may initiate action against infringement.

284. Acquiescence is one of the defences in an infringement action. The acquiescence must be sufficient to create a new right in the defendant. If the acquiescence amounts to consent, it will be a complete defence.[339]

285. Section 34 outlines that the scheme of the Act is such where rights of the prior user are recognized to be superior to that of the registration, and even the registered proprietor cannot disturb/interfere with the rights of the prior user. According to the provision, a proprietor of a trademark does not have the right to prevent the use by another party of an identical or similar mark where that user commenced prior to the user or date of registration of the proprietor. The 'first user' as discussed in the Act is a seminal part of the Act. The rights of the prior user and the registered owner of a trademark are co-extensive.[340]

286. Section 35 of the Trademarks Act, 1999, disentitles a proprietor of a registered trademark to interfere with any bona fide use by a person of his own name. According to the provisions of section 35, the proprietor or a registered user of a registered trademark cannot interfere with any bona fide use by a person of his/her

339. Power Control Appliances v. Sumeet Machines Pvt Ltd (1994) 2 SCC 448, 457.
340. P.M. Diesels Pvt Ltd v. Thukral Mechanical Works Air 1988 Del 282.

own name or that of his/her place of business, or of the name or the place of business of any of his/her predecessors in business, or the description of the character or quality of his/her goods or services.[341]

341. Arun Jaitley v. Network Solutions Pvt. Ltd. (2011) 47 PTC 1 (Del); Precious Jewels v. Varun Gems (2013) 53 PTC 233 (Del).

Chapter 7. Use of Trademarks

287. There are special provisions to deal with cases where a registered trademark is not used by the proprietor. The word 'use' means use of the mark within India. If a trademark is not used in India, it would be a ground for its removal from the Register of Trademarks.[342]

288. Use is defined in section 2(2) of the Act as a visual representation of the mark on the goods or services or in any other relation to such goods and services.

289. The meaning and scope of use have been enlightened in various judicial precedents, and any promotional material could be interpreted as use and the actual trademark use on goods and services is not a prerequisite for use. The use of a mark in relation to goods is to be construed as a reference to the use of the mark upon, or in any tangible or in any relation whatsoever, and does not necessarily be limited to physical use on goods or to the sale of goods bearing the Trademark.[343]

290. Section 46 provides for the registration and proposed use of a trademark by a company that is yet to be formed. It states that an application for the registration of a trademark shall not be refused only because it appears that the applicant has no plans to use the mark but intends to transfer such mark to a company to be formed under the Companies Act, 1956, or the proprietor intends it to be used by a person, as a registered user after the registration of the trademark. On the Registrar being satisfied about the bona fides of the applicant, registration may be granted. However, unless the company registers itself as the proprietor of the Trademark within the period specified or allowed by the Registrar, the registration shall cease to have effect and the Register shall be amended accordingly.[344]

291. Any person aggrieved by non-use may make an application for removal of the trademark from the register to the Registrar or the Appellate Board. According to section 47, a trademark can be removed from the register where there is, or has been, no bona fide intention to use the mark and the mark has not been used up to a date one month before the date of application for removal. The applicant has to prove that there has been no bona fide use of the registered trademark for five or more years, up to three months before the date of the application.[345] Where a registered proprietor has not used the mark on the goods, his/her mere advertising of the mark would not be considered bona fide use of the mark in relation to goods.[346] The expression 'by any proprietor thereof', in section 47(1)(b), should not be restricted to the use by the proprietor himself/herself or any registered user, but

342. Aktiebalaget J.P. Vulcan v. V. Section V. Palanichamy Nadar & Anr AIR 1969 Cal 43.
343. Hardie Trading v. Addison Paints and Chemicals AIR 2003 SC 3377.
344. American Home Products Corporation v. Mac Laboratories AIR 1986 SC 137.
345. Agha Hyder v. Omar Khayyam Wineries AIR 1977 Mad 166, 168.
346. Harold Radford & Co Ltd's Application (1951) 68 RPC 221.

should be construed to include use by any other bona fide authorized user.[347] The proviso excepts cases of concurrent users, that is, where marks have been registered on proof of honest concurrent use under section 12. The proviso also gives protection where the mark was not used on certain goods for which it was registered, if it was used on goods of the same description, being goods in respect of which it was registered.

292. Where the holding company permitted use of its trademark by its subsidiary company while retaining direct control and supervision over the standards and quality of the product under an agreement, it was held, rejecting the rectification petition, that charge of non-use of the mark by the holding company under section 46(1)(b) of the Act of 1958 could not be countenanced[348] (section 46 of the Act of 1958 is now section 47 of the Act of 1999).

293. Section 47(2) refers to the imposition of territorial limitation, where non-use of the mark extends to particular localities. If a mark has not been used for a period of five years either in relation to goods in a particular place in India, other than for export from India or in relation to goods to be exported to a particular market outside India, an applicant may apply to have the registration limited so as to exclude the territory where the mark has not been used. However, the applicant must be not only a person aggrieved but also a person registered under section 12.

294. According to section 47(3), where non-use has occurred due to special circumstances in trade, an application for removal of the registered trademark from the register will not succeed. The onus is on the registered proprietor to establish exceptions to section 47(3).[349]

Thus, the intention to use a trademark sought to be registered must be genuine and real.[350] The courts have held that before directing removal of the registered trademark, the Registrar must be satisfied with the following that:

(a) the application was by a 'person aggrieved';
(b) the trademark had not been used by the proprietor for a continuous period of at least five years and three months prior to the date of the application; and
(c) there were no special circumstances which affected the use of the trademark during this period by the proprietor.

295. The provisions of section 47 of the Act of 1958, regarding defensive registration of well-known trademarks, have been deleted.

347. Cycle Corporation of India Ltd v. TI Raleigh Industries Ltd AIR 1995 Cal 73, 77; American Greetings Corp's Application (1984) 1 All ER 426.
348. Fatima Tile Works v. Sudarsan Trading Co Ltd AIR 1992 Mad 12, 24.
349. Cycle Corporation of India Ltd. v. T.I. Raleigh Industries (P.) Ltd. (1996) 9 SCC 430; Satnam Overseas v. Sant Ram & Co. (2014) 57 PTC 220 (SC).
350. American Home Products Corpn. v. Mac Laboratories (P) Ltd. (1986) 1 SCC 465; Hardie Trading Ltd. v. Addisons Paint & Chemicals Ltd. (2003) 11 SCC 92.

Chapter 8. Duration of Protection: Renewal and Termination

296. Section 25 provides for the duration, renewal and restoration of trademarks. The registration of a trademark is, at the first instance, for a period of ten years from the date of registration, which under section 23 is the date of application. It may, however, be renewed from time to time. The renewal is for a period of ten years from the date of expiration of the original registration or of the last renewal of registration.

297. An application for the renewal of registration of a trademark should be made in the prescribed form, within the prescribed period, and should be accompanied with the prescribed fee. The Registrar is under a duty to notify the registered proprietor in writing of the approaching expiration. If the application along with the fee is not deposited within the specified time, the Registrar may remove the mark from the register and the removal will take effect from the expiration of the last registration. However, the Registrar shall not remove the trademark from the register if a surcharge is paid within six months from the expiration of the last registration and shall renew the registration for a period of ten years.[351]

298. After the mark has been removed from the register, the Registrar shall, after six months and within one year from the expiration of the last registration, on receipt of a request made in that behalf, restore the mark to the register on being satisfied that it is just so to do and upon such conditions as he/she may think fit to impose. Where the mark is renewed, or restored and renewed, a notice is advertised after the registered proprietor is intimated of the fact of renewal.[352]

299. It has been held that if the trademark is not renewed when it becomes due, in accordance with the provisions of this Act, the person in whose name the trademark was registered cannot claim that he/she is the registered trademark owner. If the said owner deposits the fee and the matter remains pending with the Registry of Trademarks for renewal of the trademark, then the person in whose name the trademark stands registered does not lose proprietary rights in the registered trademark on account of any delay taking place in the Registry in renewing the trademark.[353]

300. A trademark may have been removed from the register, but for the purpose of any application for the registration of another trademark during one year next after the date of the removal, the mark is deemed to be a trademark on the register, unless the Registrar is satisfied that there has been no bona fide trade use of the trademark for two years before removal, or that no deception or confusion would arise by reason of any previous use of the trademark which has been removed.[354]

351. Section 25(3).
352. Section 25(4).
353. M/s. Thapsons Pvt Ltd v. M/s. Ashoka Food Industries AIR 1992 Del 11, 13; Malhotra Book Depot v. Union of India (2012) 49 PTC 354 (Del); Cipla Limited v. Registrar of Trade Marks (2013) 56 PTC 217 (Bom).
354. Section 26, See Whirlpool Corporation v. Registrar of Trade Marks (1998) 8 SCC 1.

The Government has introduced a new custom recordation system, which permits trademark owners to record their brands and trademarks with the Ministry and take appropriate action if any counterfeit good is found at the port.[355]

355. INDIAN CUSTOMS IPR RECORDATION PORTAL, https://ipr.icegate.gov.in/IPR/homePage.

Chapter 9. Well-Known Trademarks

301. Recognition of Foreign Well-Known Marks & Transborder Reputation: The Indian courts have recognized the transborder reputation of foreign trademarks and trade names and the importance of their protection. The case *N. R. Dongre v. Whirlpool Corporation*[356] can be stated as being the first case to recognize the concept of transborder reputation of trademarks. The matter in contention was the usage of the name Whirlpool by an Indian entity which had set up an establishment of selling washing machines under the above-stated name. The respondent in the matter, i.e., Whirlpool Corporation and its Indian JV TVS Whirlpool, asserted their claim of having prior use over this mark as well as the fact that it had a transboundary reputation. They followed it by stating that goods marketed with the name Whirlpool would be deemed as being products of the respondent company and thus the washing machines sold by the appellant would give potential customers the indication that they are manufactured and sold by the respondent and thus cause confusion.

The Whirlpool Corporation sought a temporary injunction against the appellant's use of the mark, which was granted by the Delhi High Court and upheld by the Supreme Court of India. In later years, this judgment has been relied on in numerous cases. Thus, international trademarks which have no actual presence in India can ensure a protection of their mark if a transborder reputation with respect to such trademarks can be shown to exist in India. Subsequently, marks such as Volvo, Caterpillar, and Ocuflox have received protection of their trademarks via judicial decisions.

However, the applicability of the transboundary principle can also work against international trademarks if they lack the requisite transborder reputation within India, as it happened in the *Toyota Jidosha Kabushiki Kaisha v. M/S Prius Auto Industries Limited*[357] where one of the issues in question was whether the term 'Prius' could be said to have transborder reputation in India and thus provide for the appellants to have control over it. The Supreme Court stated in the negative upon finding the mark in question did not have the necessary transborder reputation as asserted by the appellants.

Rule 124 under the Trade Mark Rules 2017 allows for the registrar to declare whether a mark may be deemed as being well known or not upon an application being made by the trademark owner under Form TM-M. This procedure is a departure from the previous procedure under section 11 of the Trademarks Act, 1999, wherein a decisive statement on the well-known nature of the mark could only be made by the court or the registrar during the course of the opposition, rectification or infringement proceedings.

---

356. N. R. Dongre and Others v. Whirlpool Corporation and Another 1996 (2) ARBLR 488 SC.
357. Toyota Jidosha Kabushiki Kaisha v. M/S Prius Auto Industries Limited C/S Nos 5375–5377 OF 2017.

Chapter 10. Domain Names

302. Over the years, Indian courts have become proactive in granting protection against domain name infringements. For instance, in cases such as the *Yahoo* case,[358] courts have recognized that 'the domain name serves the same function as a trademark, and is not a mere address or like finding the number on the internet, and therefore, it is entitled to equal protection as a trademark'. With an increasing number of cases,[359] it is the need of the time that a separate registration mechanism be adopted for domain names rather than protecting them via trademarks.

358. Yahoo India v. Akash Arora (1999) PTC 201 (Del).
359. Rediff Communications Limited v. Cyberbooth AIR 2000 Bom 27. and Satyam Infoway Ltd. v. Sifynet Solutions Pvt. Ltd. AIR 2004 SC 3540 among others.

Chapter 11. Infringement and Remedies

303. Infringement: Section 29 deals with infringement of registered trademarks. It states that a registered trademark may be said to be infringed by a person who, not being the registered proprietor of the trademark or a registered user thereof, uses in the course of trade a mark which is identical with, or deceptively similar to the trademark, in relation to any goods or services in respect of which the trademark is registered and in such manner as to render the use of the mark likely to be taken as being used as a trademark.

304. Section 29 of the Act of 1999 lays down that a registered trademark is infringed if:

– the mark is identical and is used in respect of similar goods or services;[360]
– the mark is similar to the registered trademark and there is an identity or similarity of the goods or services covered by the trademark; or
– the trademark is identical and is used in relation to identical goods or services; and that such use is likely to cause confusion on the part of the public or is likely to be taken to have an association with the registered trademark. In cases falling under this category, there will be a legal presumption of likelihood of confusion on the part of the public.[361]

305. Section 29 also lays down that a registered trademark is infringed by a person if he/she uses a mark which is identical or similar to the trademark but on goods or services which are not similar, provided the registered trademark has a reputation in India and the use of the mark without due cause would take unfair advantage of or is detrimental to the distinctive character or repute of the registered trademark. It prevents a person from adopting someone else's trademark as part of that person's trade name or business name by explicitly providing that such action shall also constitute an infringement under this Act.

306. In a case of infringement of a registered trademark, or one of its essential features, the defendant cannot claim that he/she has incorporated additional material in its mark, including a description thereon of its own brand name or the name of the manufacturer conspicuously. Incorporation of 'additional material' may be a good defence in a passingoff action if the goods in question are clearly distinguished as the defendant's goods by incorporation of such additional material on the impugned mark.[362]

---

360. Parle Products (P) Ltd. v. J.P. and Co. (1972) 1 SCC 618; Mex Switchgears Pvt. Ltd. v. Max Switchgears Pvt. Ltd. (2014) 58 PTC 136.
361. Allied Blenders & Distillers Pvt. Ltd. v. Shree Nath Heritage Liquor Pvt. Ltd. (2014) 59 PTC 42 (Del); S. Oliver Bernd Frier Gmbh. & Co. Kg. v. Rasul Exports (2014) 57 PTC 475 (Del).
362. Hindustan Lever Ltd, Bombay v. Nirma Pvt Ltd AIR 1992 Bom 195, 201; Lakhara & Co v. Shivkaran Bhanwarlal Kila AIR 1994 Raj 17, 20.

307. The courts have held that statutory law relating to infringement of trademarks was based on the same fundamental principles as the general law relating to passing off and that a suit for an injunction restraining the defendant from marketing goods under a mark deceptively similar to the plaintiff's mark could be amended into one for infringement of the trademark if the plaintiff had, after the institution of the suit, obtained registration of the mark and that such an amendment would not change the cause of action but would only be in the nature of providing an alternative relief.[363]

308. Section 134 states that all suits for infringement of a registered trademark or suits relating to any right in a registered trademark or for passing off shall not be instituted in any court inferior to a District Court having jurisdiction to try the suit.

309. Remedies: Section 135 sets out reliefs that are available under the Act, in suits for infringement or for passing off. The court may grant an injunction, subject to such terms as it thinks fit, and at the option of the plaintiff, either damages or an account of profits, together with or without any order for delivery up of the infringing labels and marks for destruction or erasure, in any suit for infringement or for passing off. The order of injunction may include an ex parte injunction or any interlocutory order for discovery of documents or for preserving infringing goods, documents, etc., related to the subject matter of the suit or for restraining the defendant from disposing of his/her assets in a manner that may adversely affect the plaintiff's ability to recover any damages, etc., from the defendant.[364]

310. However, in a suit for infringement of a certification trademark, the court will not grant relief by way of damages or an account of profits. Similarly, no damages or account of profits shall be allowed by a court where the defendant has satisfied the court that at the time he/she commenced use of the trademark complained of in the suit, he/she was unaware of and had no reasonable ground for believing that the trademark of the plaintiff was registered or that the plaintiff was a registered user of the trademark. Further, when he/she became aware of the existence and nature of the plaintiff's right in the trademark, he/she forthwith ceased to use the trademark in relation to goods in respect of which it was registered.[365]

311. Temporary injunction must be granted when there is clear infringement of the plaintiff's registered trademark.[366] The word 'Don' by the defendant was held to be prima facie infringing the plaintiff's registered trademark 'Dawn' on hosiery goods.[367]

---

363. A.A. Karim Saahib v. A. Shanmugha Mudaliar (1967) 2 MLJ 468; United Breweries Ltd. v. Khodays Breweries Ltd. (2013) 55 PTC 513 (Kar).
364. Tata Sons Limited v. Gina Kilindo & Ors. (2014) 57 PTC 415; Stiefel Laboratories v. Ajanta Pharma Ltd. (2014) 59 PTC 24 (Del).
365. Section 135(3). See also Fena Limited v. Fina Europe (2013) 55 PTC 285 (Del); U. Varadaraya Nayak v. S.K. Anand (2014) 57 PTC 9 (Del).
366. Kedar Nath v. Monga Perfumery & Flour Mills AIR 1974 Del 12; Philip Morris Belgium SA v. Golden Tobacco Co Ltd AIR 1986 Del 145, 148. See Essel Packaging Ltd v. Essel Tea Exports Ltd AIR 1998 Bom 102 wherein interim injunction was granted on the ground that the members of the

312. The plea of ignorance of the plaintiff about infringement of the registered trademark does not give any right to the defendants to continue to infringe the trademark, and delay would not be fatal to the maintainability of a suit for injunction.[368]

313. The priority in adoption and use of the trademark is superior to priority in registration. To succeed in an application for temporary injunction, the plaintiff has to establish the use of the trademark prior in point of time than the impugned use by the defendant.[369] The plaintiff is entitled to choose between damages and account of profits after the liability of the defendant has been decided by the court.[370]

314. If, in an infringement action, the defendant claims honest concurrent use, he/she should make an application for the registration of his/her trademark. Where a prima facie case is made out, the court should adjourn the suit until the defendant's application is disposed.[371] It may, however, be pointed out that when the only question is whether the defendant's trademark is deceptively similar to the plaintiff's trademark, the suit should not be adjourned, even though the defendant may have made an application to register his/her trademark.[372] Infringement of a registered trademark, carried on from time to time, would give a recurring cause of action to the holder of the trademark. Therefore, whether the earlier infringement has continued or a new infringement has taken place, cause of action for filing a suit would obviously arise in favour of the plaintiff who is aggrieved by such fresh infringements of the trademark or the fresh passing off activity alleged against the defendant.[373] There have been several cases involving action against cybersquatters. The Judges have been active in protecting the owners of global brands from cybersquatting. Registration of domain names similar to international brands has been struck down, and action has been taken against the persons responsible for registering the misleading name.

---

public were misled by the use of the word 'ESSEL' in the corporate name of the defendants. See also Kirloskar Diesel Recon Pvt Ltd v. Kirloskar Pty Ltd AIR 1996 Bom 49.

367. Rupa & Co Ltd v. Dawn Mills Co Ltd AIR 1998 Guj 247.
368. Revlon Inc v. Hosiden Laboratories (India) and Os AIR 1991 NOC 77 (Delhi).
369. Century Traders v. Roshan Lal Duggar & Co AIR 1978 Del 250; M/s. Kisan Industries v. M/s. Punjab Food Corpn AIR 1983 Del 387, 391; Srisai Agencies Pvt Ltd v. Chintale Rama Rao AIR 1998 AP 86.
370. Re Eno's Case (1940) 42 Bom LR 924, 935.
371. K.C. Das Pvt. Ltd. v. K.C. Dass (2011) 48 PTC 161.
372. Adinarayana v. Brooke Bond Tea India Ltd AIR 1960 Mys 142.
373. Bengal Waterproof Ltd v. The Bombay Waterproof Manufacturing Co (1997) 1 SCC 99. 110.

Chapter 12. Overlapping and Relation to Other Intellectual Property Laws

Trademark and Geographical Indicators

315. Areas of overlap are dealt with in section 25 of the Geographical Indications of Goods Act, 1999; the Registrar of Trademarks may refuse or invalidate registration of a trademark which contains a geographical indication with respect to a good or class of goods not originating in the region indicated in the name or trademark. Any prior use of a geographical indication in good faith and without any intent to confuse or mislead and where use of the mark was before the commencement of the Geographical Indications Act, 1999, would be protected.

Part IV. Trade Names and the Action for Passing Off

Chapter 1. Sources – Legislation

316. The law governing trademarks and trade names is the Trademarks Act, 1999. This replaced the Trade and Merchandise Marks Act of 1958 (Act of 1958), along with the Trade and Merchandise Marks Rules of 1959. The 1999 Act provides for registration and better protection of trademarks for goods and services and for the prevention of the use of fraudulent marks. With the coming into force of the Act of 1999, the definition of 'mark' as per section 2(1)(m) includes a device, brand, heading, label, ticket, name, signature, word, letter, numeral, shape of goods, packaging or combination of colours or any combination thereto.

317. Passing off is dealt with under section 27. Since there is no distinction drawn between a trademark and a trade name in the Indian context, the provisions relating to passing off apply equally to trade names and trademarks.

318. According to section 27, the proprietor of an unregistered trademark (which includes a trade name) can take no action for infringement thereof. However, an exception to this rule is made where any person is passing off his/her goods or services as the goods of another person or the services provided by another person. The proprietor of a trademark/name can take action against any person for passing off his/her goods as the goods of the proprietor, even though the proprietor's trademark/name may not be registered under the Act of 1958.[374] Thus, the remedy against passing off is an independent remedy and is available even to those who are the proprietors of unregistered trademarks because registration does not create a trademark.

374. Reuter v. Muhlens (1953) 70 RPC 102; Cheddi LI v. Shakuram Bibi AIR 1967 All 269; M/s. Manoj Plastic India v. M/s. Bhola Plastic Industries AIR 1984 Del 441, 444.

Chapter 2. The Action for Passing Off

319. A passing off action is essentially an action in tort. The objective, which is based on economic policy, is to encourage enterprise, protect commercial goodwill, ensure commercial stability and ensure that people's business reputations are not exploited or encroached upon. What is protected is an economic asset.[375] No person is entitled to represent his/her goods as the goods of another person, and no person is permitted to use any mark, sign or symbol, device or other means, whereby, without making a direct false representation, he/she enables a purchaser to tell a lie or to make a false representation to somebody else who is the ultimate customer.[376] The onus, in an action for passing off, lies upon the plaintiff to establish the existence of a business reputation.

320. The tort of passing off now extends to descriptive material such as slogans or visual images on television, radio or newspaper advertising campaigns which can lead the mark to be associated with the plaintiff's product, provided that such descriptive material has become part of the goodwill of the product, in addition to trademarks and names. The test is whether the product has derived, from the advertising, a distinctive character that the market recognizes.[377]

321. The modern tort of passing off has five elements:

(1) a misrepresentation;
(2) which is calculated to injure the business or goodwill of another trader;
(3) made by a trader in the course of trade;
(4) to his/her prospective customers or ultimate consumers of goods or services supplied by him/her; and
(5) which causes actual damage to a business or goodwill of the trader by whom the action is brought.[378]

322. These elements were reiterated in many cases.[379]
The landmark cases of *Bollinger*,[380] *Vine Products*[381] and *John Walker v. Henry Ost & Co Ltd*[382] deal with the subject of passing off, which may be said to be a form of unfair trading giving rise to unlawful competition.

---

375. Ellora Industries v. Banarasi Dass AIR 1980 Del 254, 256.
376. Singer Manufacturing Co. v. Loog (1880) 18 Ch.D. 395.
377. Cadbury Schweppes Pty Ltd v. Pub Squash Co Pty Ltd [1981] 1 All ER 213.
378. Lord Diplock in Erven Warnik Besloten Vennootschap v. J. Townsend & Sons (Hull) Ltd [1979] AC 731, [1979] 2 All ER 927, 932–933; BK Engineering Co v. UBHI Enterprises AIR 1985 Del 210; M/s. Kala Niketan v. M/s. Kalaniketan AIR 1983 Del 161.
379. Cadila Health Care Ltd. v. Cadila Pharmaceutical Limited (2001) 5 SCC 73; Heinz Italia v. Dabur India Ltd. (2007) 6 SCC 1.
380. [1960] Ch 262.
381. [1969] RPC 1.
382. [1970] 2 All ER 105.

323. An applicant, for an action based on passing off, must prove the following that:[383]

- the trademark which he/she has been using on the goods manufactured by him/her has assumed a vendible character;
- he/she has been using the said trademark from before it was used by the defendant;
- his/her goods are identified and recognized by the use of the said trademark, and in case the defendant is allowed to use the said trademark or a trademark which is deceptively similar to the said trademark, it is likely to cause irreparable loss and damage to him/her; and
- there is every likelihood that the impugned trademark will invade and offend the proprietary rights of the applicant.

324. The defendant cannot escape liability for misrepresentation or actionable wrong of passing off, that is, causing injury to the plaintiff's business reputation and goodwill, merely because while describing his/her own products, the defendant partly states the truth and then mixes up the same with colourable devices, marks, words or descriptions with which the product has no natural association. In the case of a drink called 'Advocaat', the defendants did not represent their goods as goods of the plaintiffs, but it was held by the House of Lords that action was maintainable, not in its classic form of a trader representing his/her own goods as the goods of somebody else, but in an extended form.[384]

Where there is possibility of confusion in business, an injunction will be granted, despite the fact that the defendants may have adopted the name innocently.[385] The doctrine of passing off absolutely despises any form of imitation, explicit or implicit, if calculated to deceive or cause confusion in relation to trademarks.[386]

325. The Bata Shoe Company filed a passing off action against the defendant, who was using 'Bata' as a trademark on lungis (Indian sarongs) and handkerchiefs. The District Judge granted an interim injunction, but, in the appeal by the defendant, the High Court dissolved the injunction and observed that there could be no passing off unless the defendants' goods were the same as the plaintiff's goods or the defendant's goods have some connection with the plaintiff's goods. The plaintiff appealed to the Supreme Court, and by consent, the above decision was set aside, and interim injunction was granted for one month, during which period the court heard the case and, in a reasoned judgment, granted the injunction prayed for. That judgment was not appealed against.[387]

326. The plaintiffs, who were manufacturers of hosiery goods including ganjies (vests), under the trademark 'Moti', brought an action for passing off against the

383. Vinnay Chawla v. M/s. Chandamama Toytronix Pvt Ltd AIR 1992 Del 234.
384. Erven Warnik BV v. Towsend & Sons (Hull) Ltd [1980] RPC 31, 91; see also Scotch Whisky Association v. Pravara Sahakar Karkhana Ltd AIR 1992 Bom 294.
385. Laxmikant Patel v. Chetanbhai Shah (2002) 3 SCC 65.
386. Cadilla Healthcare Ltd. v. Gujarat Cooperative Milk Federation Ltd. (2008) 36 PTC 168 (Del).
387. Rustom Ali Molla v. Bata Shoe Co AIR 1957 Cal 120.

defendants for selling ganjies of a different manufacturer, under the name 'Sacha Moti'. The defendants pleaded that the word 'Moti' was their partner's father's name, and that the plaintiffs had no right to the exclusive use of the word 'Moti' and that phonetically, 'Moti' and 'Sacha Moti' were not similar. This plea was rejected by the court, and injunction, as prayed for, was granted. It was held that the question has to be approached from the point of view of a man of 'average intelligence and imperfect recollection'.[388]

While elaborating on the distinction between infringement and passing off, the Supreme Court held that while an action for passing off is a common law remedy being in substance an action for deceit, i.e., passing off by a person of his own goods as those of another, it is not the basis of the infringement. The action for infringement is a statutory remedy conferred on the registered proprietor of a registered trademark for the vindication of the exclusive right to the use of the trademark in relation to those goods.[389]

327. In an action for passing off, wherever and whenever a fresh deceitful act is committed, the aggrieved would have a fresh cause of action.[390] The remedies available in an action for passing off include injunction, damages or account of profits.

388. EEH Mills v. AT Mills AIR 1971 Cal 3.
389. Durga Dutt v. Navaratna Laboratories, AIR 1965 SC 980.
390. Bengal Water Proof Ltd v. Bombay Water Proof Mfg. Co & Ors AIR 1997 SC 1398.

Part V. Confidential Information and Trade Secrets

Chapter 1. Sources – Legislation

328. In India, there is no specific legislation that deals with confidential information and trade secrets. Remedy for breach of faith in relation to information or know-how that is meant to be confidential has to be sought in the law of contracts and in equity. In order to protect trade secrets and confidential information, watertight agreements should be agreed upon which are supported by sound policies and procedures. State secrets, however, are protected under the Official Secrets Act.

329. Confidential information is not property in any normal sense, but equity will restrain its transmission to another in breach of some confidential relationship.[391] It is treated as property by those who deal in technical know-how. Agreements for the transfer of know-how usually require the know-how supplied to be confidential.

330. Lord Denning M.R. stated in *Seager v. Copydex Limited*[392] that the law on this subject does not depend on any implied contract. It depends on the broad principles of equity that he/she who has received information in confidence shall not take unfair advantage of it. The use of such information will amount to unauthorized use of the labour of another person and thus provides a 'spring board' by which an infringer may obtain an unfair advantage over competitors.

391. Bourdman v. Phipps [1967] 21 AC 46.
392. [1967] 2 All ER 415; [1967] RPC 349.

Chapter 2. The Protection of Confidential Information

331. It has been held with regard to confidential information that the possessor of such information must be placed under a special disability in the field of competition in order to ensure that he/she does not get an unfair start.[393]

332. If the agreement is in writing for the transfer of intellectual property, maintenance of confidentiality could be a specific clause, and its violation could mean breach of contract. The obligation to keep certain information confidential is an express term of a contract. This is usually the case where there is an agreement for the transfer of know-how. The purpose of a know-how licence, as it is commonly called, is to permit the licensee or transferee to make use of the information provided for the purposes of his/her own business. Normally, the agreement will limit the degree to which the 'know-how' can be imparted to others, and use by the licensee after termination of the licence may also be circumscribed.[394]

333. The jurisdiction to restrain breach of confidence has its roots in equity, as it involves breach of trust and also because the remedy most commonly sought is injunction. The courts have now recognized a wider equitable jurisdiction, based not so much on property or on contract, but rather on good faith.[395] The findings in the '*Saltman*' case contain four important statements, which are as follows:

(1) If two parties make a contract under which one of them obtains for the purpose of the contract, or in connection with it, some confidential matter then, even though the contract is silent on the matter of confidence, the law will imply an obligation to treat such confidential matter in a confidential way, that is, one of the implied terms of the contract.
(2) If a defendant is proved to have used confidential information, obtained directly or indirectly from a plaintiff, without the consent, express or implied, of the plaintiff, he/she will be guilty of an infringement of the plaintiff's right.
(3) It would not matter in the least whether there was a contract; whether there is in existence a contract or not, it is enough if the defendants get possession over the drawings, knowing then or shortly afterwards, that they belonged to the plaintiffs and that they were obviously confidential matter, and that they had got possession for a strictly limited purpose.
(4) Information, to be confidential, must, apart from the contract, have the necessary quality of confidence about it; in other words, it must not be something which is public property and public knowledge.

---

393. Cranleigh Precision Engg Ltd v. Bryant [1964] 3 All ER 289; [1966] RPC 81.
394. National Broach v. Churchill [1965] RPC 61; Torring Low v. Smith [1966] RPC 285; Mechanical & General Inventions Co. Ltd. v. Lehwess & Austin Motor Co. (1935) AC 346.
395. Saltman Engg. Co Ltd v. Campbell Engg. Co Ltd [1948] 65 RPC 203 (CA) Relied in Zee Telefilms Ltd and Film and Shot and Anr. v. Sundial Communications Pvt Ltd and Others 2003 (27) PTC 457 Bom; see also Pepsi Foods Limited and Ors. v. Bharat Coca Cola Holdings Pvt Ltd and Ors. 81 (1999) DLT 122.

334. For a breach of confidence to be actionable, the conditions to be fulfilled are as follows:[396]

- The information transferred must have the necessary quality of confidence about it.
- The information must have been imparted in circumstances importing an obligation of confidence.
- There must be an unauthorized use of that information to the detriment of the party communicating it.

335. Confidential obligation is apparent when one person supplies information to another on the condition that he/she will keep it secret or is inferred where a person employs or requests the other to acquire information and hold it in confidence for him/her and he/she accepts that information is to be treated confidentially. If it could reasonably be believed that the information is given to the recipient, this should suffice to impose upon the recipient an equitable obligation of confidence.[397]

336. With regard to an employer-employee relationship in matters relating to confidential information, the common law is that if an employee makes an invention in the course of employment, under a contract of service or apprenticeship, all rights in such invention belong to the employer.[398] This is, of course, subject to any agreement to the contrary. The information, which is in public domain, or voluntarily revealed or insufficiently guarded, does not enjoy protection.

Trade Secret Law and Overlap with Non-personal Data Regulation

337. The Indian government's decision to explore the possibility of regulating non-personal data and potentially deriving economic gains out of it might lead to an overlap with the conceptualization of Trade Secrets.[399] Many modern-day companies are reliant on the data obtained to provide different kinds of services ranging from transport, logistics, shipping and delivery services. So far, the committee constituted to explore this issue has not stated there being any overlaps between data-sharing mechanisms and trade secrets; however, there is no clarity on the boundaries of protection offered by these rights in the context of data.

338. There is an ardent need for clarification of the overlaps between these two domains on the issue of data so as to avoid two scenarios.[400] One being the erosion

396. Coco v. Clark [1969] RPC 41; Michael Heath Nathan Johnson v. Subhash Chandra and Others 60 (1995) DLT 757.
397. Coco v. Clark [1969] RPC 41.
398. Patchett v. Sterling [1955] 72 RPC 50 (HL).
399. Report by the Committee of Experts on Non-Personal Data Governance Framework (16 Dec. 2020) – https://ourgovdotin.files.wordpress.com/2020/12/revised-report-kris-gopalakrishnan-committee-report-on-non-personal-data-governance-framework.pdf.
400. Esya Center, Response to the Second Draft Report by the Committee of Experts on Non-personal Data Governance Framework (31 Jan. 2021).

of competitive incentive structures which are crucial for private-sector-led innovation, and the second being the harm to domestic start-up ventures which would be unable to make use of data to scale across domestic and global markets.

339. In the case of a breach of confidence of confidential information or trade secrets, the remedies usually consist of an injunction, damages or an account of profits and a delivery up. The remedy granted would depend on the facts and circumstances of each individual case.[401] An injunction may be permanent or temporary. An interim injunction may also be granted. The damages awarded would be based on the market value of the confidential information.

https://www.esyacentre.org/documents/2022/4/4/response-to-the-second-draft-report-by-the-committee-of-experts-on-non-personal-data-governance-frameworkhttps://www.esyacentre.org/responses-to-public-consultations.

401. Star India Pvt Ltd v. Laxmiraj Nayan and Another 2003(3) Bom CR 563.

Part VI. Industrial Designs

Chapter 1. Sources – Legislation

340. In India, designs are protected under the Designs Act, 2000, which replaced the Designs Act, 1911. The statement of objects and reasons states that it is an Act to consolidate and amend the law relating to the protection of designs.

341. According to section 15 of the Copyright Act, 1957, any design registered under the Designs Act, 1911, will not be eligible for protection under the Copyright Act, even though it may be an original artistic work. Where a design that is eligible for protection as a design is not registered, it will be granted limited protection under the Copyright Act, 1957. This protection will cease as soon as the article to which the design has been applied has been reproduced more than fifty times, by any industrial process, by the owner of the copyright or his/her licensee as stated in section 15(2) of the Copyright Act, 1957.

342. The Locarno Classification, as established by the Locarno Agreement (1968), is an international classification used for the purposes of the registration of industrial designs. In 2019, India acceded to this agreement and became the fifty-seventh country to be a member of this agreement.[402] In furtherance of the above, the Design Rules, 2001, were amended with the introduction of the Design (Amendment) Rules, 2021.[403] While India has recently acceded to this agreement, however the first attempt at aligning India with international classifications was way back in 2008 when the Design Rules were amended to align them with the tenth Locarno Classification.[404]

343. India's accession to this agreement will among other things ensure greater unanimity with international classifications, as well as being able to play a role in determining and changing the order of classifications used. Over a period of time,

402. Locarno Notification No. 70, Ascension by Republic of India (7 Jun. 2019) https://www.wipo.int/treaties/en/notifications/locarno/treaty_locarno_70.html.
403. Government of India Notification (F.No. 5/32/2007-IPR-V) https://ipindia.gov.in/writereaddata/Portal/Images/pdf/1_26_1_design-rules-2008.pdf.
404. WIPO Press Release (7 Jun. 2019) https://www.wipo.int/portal/en/news/2019/article_0021.html.

this move among others will play a role in improving India's rankings in the Global Innovation Index and generally projecting it to be among the best centres of commerce in the world.[405]

344. The relevant design authority in India is the Office of the Controller General of Patents, Designs and Trademarks, headquartered in Kolkata, which processes all applications for designs filed anywhere in India under the Designs Act, 2000, and the Design Rules, 2001.

345. A 'design' is defined as 'the features of shape, configuration, pattern or ornament or composition of lines or colour or combination thereof applied to any article whether two-dimensional or three-dimensional or in both forms, by any industrial process or means, whether manual, mechanical or chemical, separate or combined, which in the finished article appeal to and are judged solely by the eye'. A 'design' does not include mechanical devices. Thus, any mark under section 479 of the Indian Penal Code, 1860, or artistic work under section 2(c.)of the Copyright Act, 1957, is not protected as designs.

346. A design needs to be a new and original work which has not been published in India or overseas. Original works are protected as are anything that has been applied in a new context to an article. *Indian Design Law follows* the class and subclass under the Locarno Classification and will not cover a mere mechanical device. The design becomes eligible for registration, provided that:

– it is new or original;
– it has not been disclosed by prior publication or use or in any other way;
– it is sufficiently distinguishable from known designs or their combination; and
– it is not contrary to public order or morality and is not scandalous or obscene in any manner.

347. The amendments to the Design Rules (made from time to time) are aimed at modernizing and simplifying the registration process for industrial designs. Electronic filing is allowed along with processes to allow online filing and tracking of applications. The fees for individuals, small entities and start-ups have been reduced to make the process affordable for emerging businesses. The definition of Design has been expanded to include new forms of creative expression such as Graphical User Interfaces (GUIs) and typographic arrangements. The adoption of the Locarno Classification aligns India's design laws with international standards. Further legislative inclusion is needed for spare parts which often feature unique designs that are integral to the overall product. The subjective nature of the registration process for determining what constitutes originality should be streamlined as well.

405. Yashi Agrawal, India's Accession to the Locarno Agreement: Amendments to the Design Rules, 2001 & Other Impacts, SPICY IP (28 Jul. 2021) https://spicyip.com/2021/07/indias-accession-to-the-locarno-agreement-amendments-to-the-design-rules-2001-other-impacts.html.

348. Once a design application is filed, it is subject to a first examination and a report is normally published within a month. In case objections are raised, the Design Office investigates the claims and may call the parties for personal hearings. They examine seven photographic views including: perspective view; front view; back view; top view; bottom view; left view; and right view, and clear line drawing. This process usually takes about a year. The protection is only within the territory of India. A six-month grace period is available on prior notification to the Controller of Designs *in case of participation of the Design in* an exhibition or trade show. The provisions contained in the Paris Convention on the right of priority are applicable and an application in India must be filed within six months from the date of convention filing. The design is generally published within fifteen days after the design is accepted.

349. After publication, it is open to the public and cannot be kept secret. Deferment of a design publication is possible only during the examination stage. *Registration may be refused, inter alia,* for prior publication. The applicant needs to differentiate its application from prior designs and designs applied for registration and file a reply addressing each objection. In case the Controller of Designs refuses an application, appeal lies to the High Court of Calcutta within three months from the date of the order of refusal. When a design is accepted and registered, a certificate of registration is issued to the applicant. The articles where the design is used may be marked as 'REGD.' or 'REGISTERED', with or without the registration number to prevent others from dealing with products which have an identical appearance. These rights emanate from the priority date under the Paris Convention or the date of application. The term is for ten – fifteen years, and renewal may be applied for within ten years of the priority date/ date of filing. The design may be assigned on an exclusive or non-exclusive basis.

350. The Designs (Amendment) Rules, 2021 (Amendment Rules), were published in the Gazette of India on 25 January 2021 by the Department for Promotion of Industry and Internal Trade. India now follows the thirteenth Edition of the Locarno Classification as per the current edition of international classification for industrial designs by the World Intellectual Property Organization (WIPO). Start-ups recognized under the Government of India's Startup India Initiative have been expressly recognized and have discounted fees. This covers filing, prosecuting and maintaining a design application/registration in India. The Amendment Rules permit foreign entities to apply as start-ups if they declare that they meet the criterion as per the Startup India Initiative. In the case of *Ust Global (Singapore) Pte Ltd v. The Controller of Patents and another*, the High Court of Calcutta AID No. 2 of 2019 in March 2023 set aside the decision of the Controller of Designs to deny registration to Graphical User Interface (GUI) and after making observations in favour of registrability of GUI applications remanded the application back to the Controller of Designs for fresh consideration while pointing out that Designs Rules in 2019 and 2021 and Class 14.04 of the Locarno Classification specifically allows the registrability of 'Screen Displays and Icons'. Additionally, the amendments made to the Design Rules in 2021 introduced Class 32, containing graphic symbols, graphic designs, logos, ornamentation, and surface patterns. A software developer develops the source code that creates the GUI. This is then embedded in the micro-controllers/ processors and is displayed on screen by illuminating pixels by electronic means. The process was held to be an industrial process under section 2(d) of the Designs Act, and the visual appeal of the design could be displayed on any internal or external feature.

351. Anyone with a registered design certificate may enforce their rights at Indian Borders under the Intellectual Property Rights (Imported Goods) Enforcement Rules, 2007. IP rights holder may give notice to the Customs Commissioner requesting the suspension of clearance of goods suspected to be infringing their design. The Customs Department may suspend the clearance of the alleged infringing articles if they have prima facie evidence to believe the goods are counterfeit/ infringing in nature.

352. The significant developments in relation to designs in the last year are as follows:

- Submission of online forms as prescribed in the Designs Rules (as amended) digitally signed in accordance with sections 3 and 4 of the Information Technology Act, 2000, except for assignment, attested/notarized copy of the original Power of Attorney and original affidavit (if any) for e-filed applications.
- Issuance of electronic certificates of registration and renewal.
- WIPO Digital Access Service (DAS) code or priority documents in accordance with Rule 15 of the Designs Rules (as amended) are needed for reciprocal filings.

Chapter 2. Subject Matter of Protection

353. The Act protects the exclusive right of a proprietor to use a registered design. According to section 2(d), 'design' means only the features of shape, configuration, pattern or ornament applied to any article, whether in two-dimensional or three-dimensional, or both forms, by any industrial process or means, whether manually, mechanically or chemically, separate or combined, which in the finished article appeal to and are judged solely by the eye, but does not include any mode or principle of construction or anything which in substance is a mere mechanical device, and does not include any trademark, or property mark as defined in section 479 of the Indian Penal Code, or any artistic work defined in section 2(c) of the Copyright Act, 1957.

A good design must be visually appealing, though it need not be an artistic work or possess artistic merit.[406]

354. The exclusive right to the use of a registered design is known as 'copyright', and it has been defined under section 2(c) to mean the exclusive right to apply a design to any article in any class in which the design is registered.

355. A design is different from a trademark in that it is necessarily a part and parcel of the article manufactured, while a trademark is not necessarily so.[407] A label put on a carton to be used as a container for the goods can never amount to 'design' under section 2(d) of the Act.[408]

406. Parle Products Pvt. Ltd. v. Surya Food & Agro Ltd. (2009) 40 PTC 638 (Mad); Polymer Papers v. Gurmit Singh (2002) 25 PTC 327 (Del).
407. Ampro Food Products v. Ashok Biscuit Works and others AIR 1973 AP 17.
408. Hindustan Lever Limited, Bombay v. Nirma Pvt Ltd, Ahmedabad AIR 1992 Bom 195.

Chapter 3. Conditions of Protection

356. Section 4 states that an application for registration may be made by the proprietor of any 'new or original design, not previously published in any country'. The expression 'new or original' means that the design has not been made known to public and that it has been invented for the first time or it has not been reproduced by anyone else.[409] It is clear from the provisions that the essential conditions that a design must fulfil to obtain protection under the Act are that the design:

– must be new or original;[410]
– must not be previously published in India or in any other country;[411]
– must be significantly distinguishable from known designs or combination of known designs; and
– does not contain scandalous or obscene matter.

409. Bharat Glass Tube Ltd v. Gopal Glass Works Ltd (AIR 2008 SC 2520); Steelbird Hi-tech India Ltd. v. SPS Gambhir & Ors. (2014) 58 PTC 428.
410. Wimco Ltd. v. Meena Match Industries, AIR 1983 Del 537.
411. National Trading Co. v. Monica Chawla, AIR 1994 Del 309; Reckitt Benkiser v. Wyeth Ltd. (2013) 54 PTC 90 (Del).

Chapter 4. Formalities (Procedure for Grant and Obtaining Protection)

357. Section 5 provides for the formalities to be complied with in making an application for registration of a design. It states that the Controller shall, before registration of the design, refer the application for examination by an examiner appointed under section 3(2) of the Act. Upon the receipt of the report of the examiner, the Controller may either register the design or refuse to register. In the case of refusal, the decision can be appealed before the High Court. The application for registration must be made in the prescribed form and must be accompanied by the prescribed fee.

358. Section 5 also lays down that the same design may not be registered in more than one class, and in case of any doubt as to which class the design is to be registered, the Controller shall decide the question.

359. An application that does not fulfil the requirements under the Act may be deemed to be abandoned, under section 5(5) of the Act. The design, when registered, shall be registered as of the date of the application for registration.

360. Under section 9, the Controller shall grant a certificate of registration to the proprietor of the design when it is registered. In case of loss of the original certificate or in any other case, the Controller may furnish one or more copies of the certificate.

Chapter 5. Ownership and Transfer (Assignment: Licences)

361. The registered proprietor of a design may transfer ownership in such design by way of assignment, licence, mortgage, or the ownership may be transferred by operation of law in the case of transmission, as is provided for in section 30. All such transfers in ownership are required to be registered with the Controller, under an application in the prescribed form.

Chapter 6. Scope of Exclusive Rights

362. Under section 11 of the Act, a registered design will vest the copyright in the design upon the registered owner for a period of ten years in the first instance and can be renewed for a further period of five years. This includes the exclusive right to apply a design to any article in any class in which the design is registered [section 2(c) of the Designs Act, 2000].

363. Under the Designs Act, 2000, section 2(d) excludes any mode or principle of construction, anything, which is in substance a mechanical device, trademarks, property marks and artistic works. Artistic works have been excluded from the 2000 Act, while all the other exclusions are identical to the exclusions in the 1911 Act.

Further, section 4 prohibits the registration of a design, which is:

(a) not new or original;
(b) has been disclosed to the public anywhere in India or overseas by publication in a tangible form prior to the filing date or where applicable the priority date of the application;
(c) is not significantly distinguishable from known designs or combination of known designs; or
(d) comprises or contains scandalous or obscene matter.

The test for infringement is that a common man should be able to look at the original design and later at the infringement and think that they are identical, proving passing off. However, even small differences in shape, size, colour could cause an action for passing off to fail even if the design is substantially similar to the protected design.

364. Section 21 of the Act permits the exhibition of a design, or of any article to which a design is applied, at an industrial or other exhibition, whether in India or not, and does not prevent the registration of the design merely on account of such exhibition. However, the applicant for registration must make the application for registration within six months from the date of first exhibiting the design, etc.

365. The duration of protection for a registered design is ten years with an option for extension of the protection by another five years. For unregistered designs, there is limited protection under section 15 of the Copyright Act, as the protection ceases as soon as the article is reproduced more than fifty times.[412] The Designs Act, unlike the Copyright Act, gave monopoly protection in the strict sense of the word rather than mere protection against copying as under the Copyright Act. Though there was an area of overlap between the Copyright Act and the Designs Act, the two Acts did not give coterminous protection as regards the subject matter.[413]

412. Section 11, Designs Act, 2000.
413. Parle Products Pvt. Limited v. Surya Food & Agro Ltd. (2009) 40 PTC 638 (Mad).

Chapter 7. Cancellation of Design

366. Section 19 allows for any person to present a petition for a cancellation of the design registration at any point after the registration on the following grounds that: *the design has been previously registered in India; it has been published in India or in any other country prior to the registration date; the design is not a new or original design; the design is not registrable under the Designs Act or it is not a design as defined under section 2(d) of the Designs Act. An appeal from any order by the Controller can be filed with the High Court.*

Chapter 8. Infringement and Remedies

367. The provisions relating to infringement or 'piracy' of copyright in a registered design and the remedies available to the registered proprietor thereof, in case of infringement or 'piracy', are contained in section 22 of the Act.

368. Section 22 states that during the existence of the copyright in any design, it shall not be lawful for any person to do the following:

- to apply the registered design, or any fraudulent imitation thereof, to any article in any class of goods for which the design is registered for the purpose of selling such article, without a licence or written consent of the registered proprietor, or to do anything with a view to enable the design to be so applied;
- to import for the purpose of sale, without the consent of the registered proprietor, any article belonging to the class in which the design has been registered, and applying to it the design or any fraudulent or obvious imitation thereof;
- knowing that the design or any fraudulent or obvious imitation thereof has been applied to any article, in any class of goods for which the design is registered, without the consent of the registered proprietor, to publish or expose or cause to be published or exposed for sale that article.

369. As regards remedies, section 22 states that any person who acts in contravention of the above provisions shall be liable for every contravention in the following ways:

- to pay the registered proprietor of the design a sum not exceeding INR 25,000 (USD 1 = INR 64 approx.) recoverable as a contract debt, up to a maximum of INR 50,000 in respect of;
- if the proprietor so elects to pay such damages as may be awarded and be restrained by an injunction.

However, the act does not provide for any criminal actions against the infringing party.

370. When the court makes a decree in a suit for damages or an injunction, it shall send a copy of the decree to the Controller who shall cause an entry to be made in the Register of Designs. Any suit or other proceeding for relief can be instituted only in the District Court.

371. It is not necessary in the case of every design or pattern, in order to bring it within the statute, that it must be an exact reproduction of the registered design, or that the words 'fraudulent' and 'obvious imitation' in the section must be construed to mean exact reproduction.[414] The onus of proving that no infringement has occurred is on the defendant.[415] In case of infringement of a design, the plaintiff can claim the profit earnings by the defendant.[416]

372. In a suit for damages and injunction, restraining the defendant from infringing the plaintiff's copyright in respect of certain designs, the onus of proving that the defendant had knowledge of the plaintiff's right in the said design lies on the plaintiff.[417]

373. Signatories to the Paris Convention allow reciprocity for the purpose of claiming priority.

374. In *Ttk Prestige Ltd v. Kcm Appliances Private Limited* before the High Court of Delhi CS(COMM) 697/2022 in April 2023, it was held that certificate of registration for a design registered for a 'Pressure Cooker with Container and Lid (Set) for Household' with six drawings instead of one was not invalid. Design 324727-001, registered in Class 07-02, includes 'Cooking appliances, utensils, and containers'. The court noted that the term 'article' in the Designs Act encompasses any part of an article capable of being made and sold separately. Therefore, *multiple articles falling within the same class can be covered by one design registration involving the same shape and configuration.* The court held that the defendant had borrowed the idea of the design from the plaintiff and was restrained from selling the pressure cooker which infringed the suit design. In another recent judgment in *Havells India Ltd. v. Panasonic Life Solutions India Pvt Ltd. and another*, the High Court of Delhi held in Case No.: CS(COMM) 261/2022 & I.A. 6259/2022, 7226/2022 in May 2022 relied on the judgment of *Mohan Lal, Proprietor of Mourya Industries v. Sona Paint and Hardwares* (2013 SCC Online Del 1980); *Carlsberg Breweries A/S v. Som Distilleries and Breweries Ltd.* (2018 SCC Online Del 1292); and *Whirlpool of India v. Videocon Industries Ltd.* (2014 SCC Online Bom 565). On the facts of this case, the court held that the aesthetics were not similar enough to deceive the average consumer; however, *the design itself was held to be a case of infringement under section 22 of the Designs Act as while the design was not identical, it had enough resemblance* with the plaintiff's fan design to justify an injunction.

414. Dunlop Rubber Co. Ltd. v. Golf Ball Developments Ltd. (1931) 48 RPC 268; Calico Printers Association Ltd v. Swami & Co AIR 1939 Bom 103; Hindustan Sanitaryware and Industries Limited v. Dip Crafts Industries (2003) 26 PTC 163 (Del); Castrol India Ltd. v. Tide Water Oil Co. (I) Ltd. (1996) 16 PTC 202.
415. Mohamad Abdul Karim v. Mohamed Yasin & Another AIR 1934 All 798.
416. Tobu Enterprises Pvt Ltd v. Joginder Metal Works AIR 1985 Del 244; Three-N-Products Private Limited v. Manchanda Enterprises (2002) 25 PTC 607 (Cal); Polar Industries v. Usha International (2000) 20 PTC 469.
417. Calico Printers Association Ltd v. D.N. Mukherjee AIR 1936 Cal 493.

Part VII. Geographical Indications of Goods (Registration and Protection) Act, 1999

Chapter 1. Sources – Legislation

375. The Geographical Indications of Goods (Registration and Protection) Act, 1999 (G.I. Act), was enacted within the time frame stipulated to fulfil India's obligations under the TRIPS Agreement, to which it is a signatory. Before this statute was enacted, India did not have any legislation for the protection of geographical indications of goods. The provisions of the G.I. Act are largely based on the provisions of the TRIPS Agreement relating to Geographical Indications. The preamble to the G.I. Act states that it is an Act to provide for the registration and better protection of geographical indications relating to goods. Furthermore, all goods are classified in accordance with the International Classification of Goods for the purposes of G.I. registration. The said Act came into force in 2003.

376. Geographical Indications (GIs) give protection to goods that originate in a specific place. The use of the term 'Champagne' versus 'sparkling wine' may be the best known example. GIs allow a degree of protection to a specific category of goods manufactured in a particular region. The same good manufactured in another region cannot use the same name though it may be identical in composition. This protects the industry in its area of origin. The GIs are defined and given legal recognition and protection. A registered GI can prevent others from using the name and thereby prevent passing off of goods made elsewhere as the protected category. The Geographical Indications Registry in Chennai is co-located with the Controller General of Patents, Designs, and Trade Marks Office. Applicants can apply for a ten-year registration protection by filing an application which highlights the specific qualities and goodwill the product from a specific region enjoys. This is renewable.

Need for Geographical Indication Protection in India

377. India has an ancient and diverse history of making products from different materials and growing certain crops. Reputed GIs like Basmati Rice, Darjeeling Tea, Alphonso Mango, Benarasi Sarees, Kanjeevaram Silk and Pashmina are known all over the world and command a certain value from the GI; Pashmina from Kashmir commands a different price from Pashmina sourced from Himachal for instance. Similarly, Basmati rice grown in the United States (US) can be sold as 'Texmati' but not as 'Basmati'. The GI status prevents products from other territories being mislabelled as identical to the GI-protected product. Local communities benefit by being able to command higher prices and help to preserve the traditional way of life of those communities and ensuring that certain skills like specific types of weaving get passed down from generation to generation. Skilled craftsmen all over India are facing an exodus of their children. For these youths, the competition to traditional crafts, such as weaving, include becoming data entry operators. Through this, they avoid spending hours in a weaving pit in the heat. However, they also no longer contribute to producing fabrics/textiles which are a link to India's past. Both occupations earn about the same amount, but while one enriches culture, the other is a line function. Situations like these lead to skill drain in the country.

Future Prospects

378. With widespread imitation, even with GI protection, craftsmen face an uphill battle. Enforcement is weak, and there is imitation across the board. Many craftsmen are not aware of their rights in the case of the textile industry; the power loom has dealt a death blow to weavers. Handloom has become expensive, and power looms can churn out products in an instant.

379. The GI system needs to improve enforcement and crack down on unauthorized use of GIs. The registration process is cumbersome, particularly given the linguistic diversity in India and the lack of recognition of skilled craftsmen, unlike Europe where the Guilds control every vocation. Streamlining the registration process to better support small producers is needed. Strengthening the enforcement, expanding the list of registered GIs and integration systems for traceability and authentication are needed.

Chapter 2. Subject Matter of Protection

380. The exclusive right to use a geographical indication in relation to a particular class of goods, for a prescribed number of years, is the subject matter of protection under the G.I. Act. The term 'geographical indication' has been defined in section 2(1)(e) of the G.I. Act to mean an indication which identifies such goods as agricultural goods, natural goods or manufactured goods as originating, or manufactured in the territory of a country, or a region or locality in that territory, where a given quality, reputation or other characteristic of such goods is essentially attributable to its geographical origin and in case where such goods are manufactured goods, one of the activities of either the production or of processing or preparation of the goods concerned, takes place in such territory, region or locality, as the case may be. The term 'indication' has been defined in section 2(1)(g) of the G.I. Act to include any name, geographical or figurative representation or any combination of them, conveying or suggesting the geographical origin of goods to which it applies. For instance, 'Pochampally' Handloom Sari as well as the Pochampally Logo have been granted a GI Tag in the last fifteen years.[418] The sale of saris which originate from the State of Telangana had initially suffered an immense drop because of the rampant copying of their designs by mills that sold these saris at much cheaper rates.

418. GI Registration Details of Pochampally Kat, https://search.ipindia.gov.in/GIRPublic/Application/Details/4.

Chapter 3. Conditions of Protection

381. A geographical indication will be provided protection under the G.I. Act only if certain prescribed conditions are fulfilled. In the first instance, according to section 20, only a registered geographical indication will be entitled to protection. Section 8 provides for registration to be in respect of particular goods and areas. It states that a geographical indication may be registered in respect of any or all of the goods, and in respect of a definite territory of a country or region/locality, as may be prescribed. The Registrar shall classify the goods in accordance with the International Classification of Goods. Where any question arises regarding the classification of goods or the determination of the definite area, the decision of the Registrar shall be final.

382. Furthermore, section 9 prohibits the registration of certain geographical indications, the use of which would be likely to deceive or cause confusion, or which would be contrary to law, or which comprises scandalous or obscene matter, or which is likely to hurt the religious sensibilities of any class or section of the citizens of India, or which are determined to be generic names or indications and therefore cannot be protected in the country of their origin or which have fallen into disuse in that country or which, although literally true as to the territory, region or locality in which the goods originate, but falsely represent that the goods originated in another territory, regional or locality as the case may be.

383. If a geographical indication fulfils the conditions prescribed under section 20 and section 9, it will be covered by the protective clauses of the G.I. Act.

Chapter 4. Formalities: Procedure for the Grant and Obtaining Protection

384. The G.I. Act lays down certain procedures to be complied with for the registration of a geographical indication. Section 11 of the G.I. Act provides for an application to be made for the registration of a geographical indication. It states that any association of persons or producers or any organization or authority established by or under any law for the time being in force representing the interest of the producers of the concerned goods may make an application to the Registrar in such form and manner and accompanied by such fees as may be prescribed.

385. The application shall contain the following details:

(1) A statement as to how the geographical indication serves to designate the goods as originating from the concerned territory of the country, or region or locality in the country, as the case may be, in respect of specific quality, reputation and other characteristic should be essentially attributable to the geographical origin.
(2) The class of goods to which the geographical indication shall apply.
(3) The geographical map of the territory of the country or region or locality in the country in which the goods originate or are being manufactured.
(4) Particulars regarding the appearance of the geographical indication.
(5) A statement containing such particulars of the producers of the concerned goods as may be prescribed.

386. Every application for registration shall be filed in the office of the Geographical Indications Registry within whose territorial limits the territory of the country, or the region or locality in the country, to which the geographical indication relates, is situated. A single application may be made for registration of a geographical indication for different classes of goods.

387. The Registrar shall examine all applications in the manner prescribed and may refuse an application or may accept it absolutely or subject to such amendments, modifications, conditions or limitations, if any, as he/she thinks fit. Where the Registrar refuses or conditionally accepts an application, he/she shall record in writing the grounds for such refusal or conditional acceptance and the materials used by him/her in arriving at his/her decisions.

388. As per section 12 of the G.I. Act, the Registrar may withdraw his/her acceptance of the application if he/she is satisfied that the application has been accepted in error or, that in the circumstances of the case, the geographical indication should not be registered or should be registered on terms different from those on which the application has been accepted. Section 13 states that when an application for registration of a geographical indication has been accepted, the Registrar shall cause the application to be advertised in the manner prescribed.

389. Section 14 deals with opposition to the registration of a geographical indication by any person. Any person may, within three months (or such extended period, not exceeding one month, as may be allowed by the Registrar) from the date of advertisement or re-advertisement of an application for registration, oppose the registration by giving the Registrar a notice in writing in the prescribed manner. The Registrar will serve a copy of the notice on the applicant, who will send his/her counterstatement to the Registrar in the prescribed manner, within the prescribed time. The Registrar will serve a copy of this counterstatement on the person opposing the registration. The Registrar shall thereafter hear both parties and decide the matter.

Chapter 5. Ownership and Transfer

390. Section 24 of the G.I. Act expressly prohibits the transfer or assignment of a geographical indication. It states that notwithstanding anything contained in any other law for the time being in force, any right to a registered geographical indication shall not be the subject matter of assignment, transmission, licensing, pledge, mortgage or any such other agreement. The only exception to the rule is stated in the proviso to the section, when, upon the death of an authorized user, the right of the deceased in a registered geographical indication would devolve on his/her successor in title.

Chapter 6. Scope of Exclusive Rights

391. The rights conferred by the G.I. Act upon the registered proprietor and authorized user of a registered geographical indication are the right to obtain relief in respect of any infringement of the registered geographical indication and the exclusive right to the use of the geographical indication in relation to the goods in respect of which it is registered.

392. In addition, section 23 also states that in all legal proceedings relating to a geographical indication, the certificate of registration granted by the Registrar under the G.I. Act shall be prima facie evidence of the validity of the registered indication. This certificate of registration shall be admissible in all courts and before the Appellate Board.

Chapter 7. Duration and Maintenance

393. According to section 18, the registration of a geographical indication shall be for a period of ten years in the first instance. However, the registration may be renewed from time to time for a further period of ten years in accordance with the provisions of the G.I. Act.

394. Section 18 further provides that if the registered proprietor or authorized user of a geographical indication does not pay the prescribed fee or does not comply with the formalities for renewal of registration, even after receiving a notice in this regard from the Registrar, then the Registrar may remove the geographical indication from the Register. However, on an application being made by the registered proprietor or authorized user for restoration of the geographical indication to the Register, the Registrar may do so if he/she is satisfied that it is justified in the circumstances.

Chapter 8. Infringement and Remedies

395. A detailed description of the acts that constitute infringement under the G.I. Act of 1999 is given in section 22. The provisions of section 22 state that a registered geographical indication is infringed by a person who, not being an authorized user thereof:

(a) uses such geographical indication by any means in the designation or presentation of goods that indicates or suggests that such goods originate in a geographical area other than the true place of origin of such goods, in a manner which misleads the persons as to the geographical origin of such goods; or
(b) uses any geographical indication in such manner which constitutes an act of unfair competition, including passing off in respect of registered geographical indication.

396. The penalties prescribed by the G.I. Act of 1999, depending on the extent of infringement, include:

(1) injunction;
(2) damages or account of profits;
(3) delivery up of infringing material;
(4) indication of destruction or erasure;
(5) imprisonment of up to three years, with or without fine; and
(6) fines of up to INR 2 lakhs with or without imprisonment.

Part VIII. The Protection of Plant Varieties and Farmers' Rights Act, 2001

Chapter 1. Sources – Legislation

397. India has enacted the Protection of Plant Varieties and Farmers' Rights Act, 2001, in compliance with its obligations under Article 27.3(b) of the TRIPS Agreement relating to protection of plant varieties. The Act is passed for the establishment of an effective system for protection of plant varieties, the rights of farmers and plant breeders and to encourage the development of new varieties of plants. The Act was also enacted to recognize and protect the rights of the farmers in respect of their contribution made at any time in conserving, improving and making available plant genetic resources for the development of new plant varieties.

Chapter 2. Subject Matter of Protection

398. The Act provides protection for different varieties of plants.

399. The Act provides for the establishment of the 'Protection of Plant Varieties and Farmers Rights Authority (PPVFRA), set up in November 2005'. The duties and functions of the Authority, *inter alia*, include the registration of extant and new plant varieties, development of characterization and documentation of varieties, provision of compulsory licensing of protected varieties where the right holder does not arrange for production and sale of the seeds and collection of statistics with regard to plant varieties, seeds and germplasm for compilation and publication. A Registry, known as the Plant Varieties Registry, has been set up. A National Register of Plant Varieties (as stated in section 13 of the legislation) is to be kept at the head office of the Registry in which names of all registered plant varieties, along with the names and addresses of the respective breeders, the rights of such breeders and other prescribed particulars are to be entered. The Act also provides for the procedural aspects of registration of a plant variety and the persons who may make an application for such registration. In order to be eligible for protection, a plant variety must be distinct, uniform and stable.

400. In the event that an application for registration for a plant variety is registered, the Registrar thereafter issues a certificate of registration under section 23(8) of the Act (for an essentially derived variety) and section 24 (for a variety). In accordance with section 24(6), the registration certificate is valid for a period of nine years in the case of trees and vines and six years in the case of other crops. This registration while being renewable for further periods has a total period beyond which the validity cannot exceed.

401. The period of protection shall be eighteen years for trees and vines from the date of registration, fifteen years from the date of notification for extant varieties by Central Government and in the case of all other plants, it is fifteen years from the date of registration. The breeders' rights would include the breeders' authorization for production and commercial sale of the product or propagating material of a protected variety.[419]

402. In May 2016, the Ministry of Agriculture and Farmers' Welfare, Government of India, issued a notification on the Licensing and Formats for GM Technology Agreement Guidelines. These guidelines provide for the patent protection for the plant varieties carrying the GM traits under this Act.

403. Previously, the PPVFRA was also responsible for ensuring that an entity had to secure a Non-Objection Certificate from the patent holder to allow for the

419. Nishith Desai Associates, Intellectual Property Laws in India, NISHITH DESAI (July 2015), http://www.nishithdesai.com/fileadmin/user_upload/pdfs/Research%20Papers/Intellectual_Property_Law_in_India.pdf, p. 36.

use of their genetically modified (GM) traits.[420] However, this requirement was done away with as of 2017, a decision which is likely to create disputes between agrochemical giants such as Monsanto, as Monsanto's bollworm-resistant GM trait is found in almost all the GM cotton crops grown in the country. This is a significant development for Indian companies as by virtue of this notification they can now release plant varieties in the market without the prospect of controlling or withholding their release. A larger development is with regard to the reduced ability that companies like Monsanto hold in terms of controlling the market. However, this notification does not exempt the Indian companies from facing any suits due to infringement or licence breach on their part. As such, restrictive covenants on the licensing agreements are good in law at present, and any change to the position would only happen in the event the Competition Commission considers it to be anti-competitive activity.[421]

420. Vivian Fernandes, PPVFR Act Dispensing with NOCs: Agriculture Ministry Rendered Hollow the Plant Trait Patents of Companies Like Monsanto, FINANCIAL EXPRESS (21 Jun. 2017), http://www.financialexpress.com/economy/ppvfr-act-dispensing-with-nocs-agriculture-ministry-rendered-hollow-the-plant-trait-patents-of-companies-like-monsanto/728559/.

421. Prashant Reddy, NOC Requirement for Registering or Releasing New Plant Varieties Scrapped, SPICY IP (9 Jul. 2017) https://spicyip.com/2017/07/noc-requirement-for-registering-or-releasing-new-plant-varieties-scrapped.html.

Part IX. The Biological Diversity Act, 2002

404. The Biological Diversity Act, 2002, was enacted to provide for conservation of biological diversity, sustainable utilization and equitable sharing of benefits arising out of utilization of genetic resources. The Act was enacted to give effect to the provisions of the United Nations Convention on Biological Diversity, signed at Rio de Janeiro on 5 June 1992. Biological Diversity means the variability among living organisms from all sources and the ecological complexes of which they are part and includes diversity within species or between species and of ecosystems. Furthermore, it is important to note that only selective provisions of the Biodiversity Act, 2002 – namely, definition provisions, provisions relating to the constitution of the National Biodiversity Authority (NBA) and rule-making powers of Government – have been brought into force with effect from 1 October 2003.[422] The NBA is responsible for regulating the commercial/other uses of biodiversity by both Indian and Non-Indian entities.

405. Section 3 of the Act prohibits persons who are, *inter alia*:

(1) not Indian citizens;
(2) non-resident citizens of India;
(3) body corporates/associations/organizations not incorporated/registered in India, from obtaining any biological resource occurring in India or from obtaining any knowledge from such biological resource for commercial utilization or for bio-survey and bio-utilization.

406. Section 6 of the Act prohibits the grant of any IPR, whether inside or outside India, for any invention based on any research or information on a biological resource obtained in India, except with the permission of the NBA. The Act provides for the establishment of the NBA, which shall regulate the activities relating to obtaining biological resources occurring in India, or transferring the results of any research relating to that for monetary consideration,[423] or grant of any IPR for the same. It further provides for the establishment of a Biological Management Committee for the purpose of promoting conservation, sustainable use and documentation of biological diversity, including preservation of habitats, conservation of landraces, folk varieties and cultivars, domesticated stocks and breeds of animals

422. Government of India Notification (F.No.J-/22018/46/2003-CSC(BC)) http://nbaindia.org/uploaded/pdf/notification/8%20%20Sec%201%202%208%2017.pdf.
423. Section 4.

and microorganisms and chronicling of knowledge relating to biological diversity. In terms of penalties, if any person violates the provisions of section 3, 4 or 6 of the Act, then he/she can be liable to punishment of imprisonment for up to five years or a fine up to INR 10 lakhs. In addition to this, the Central Government in 2018 issued a direction under section 48 of the Biological Diversity Act, 2002. It provided for an immunity deal for individuals who may have committed any acts without the requisite approval from authorities. These individuals were permitted to file and obtain approval for past conduct without any fear of criminal prosecutions. Some commentators have reflected on the success of the aforementioned decision while also addressing the issue of the arbitrariness for deciding the benefit-sharing payments to be made by those who wish to seek approval for past conduct.[424]

424. Adarsh Ramanujan, National Biodiversity Authority Imposing Upfront Monetary Payment as Benefit Sharing for Research, SPICY IP (5 Jan. 2021) https://spicyip.com/2021/01/national-biodiversity-authority-imposing-upfront-monetary-payment-as-benefit-sharing-for-research.html.

Part X. The Semiconductor Integrated Circuits Layout-Design Act, 2000

Chapter 1. Sources – Legislation

407. India enacted the said Act to give effect to the TRIPS Agreement relating to layout-design (Topographies) of Integrated Circuit. The preamble of the Act states that the Act was passed for the protection of the semiconductor integrated circuits layout-designs and related matters. While the act was approved by both houses of the parliament, only certain provisions of the act were brought into effect in 2011.[425] This happens because of differential gradients that each of these legislations lay emphasis on. In the context of a layout-design of an IC, the concept of originality is most significant, while patent law requires ideas to be original and novel. As of 2016, the Government, vide a notification dated 17 March, transferred the administration of the Copyright Act from the HRD Ministry and that of Semiconductor Integrated Circuits Layout-Design Act from the IT Ministry to the Department of Industrial Policy & Promotion (DIPP – functioning under the Ministry of Commerce and Industry).[426] This transfer was aimed with the intention of bringing all IP offices under the control of DIPP, which previously had administrative control over the Patent and Design Office as well as those over Trade Marks and Geographical Indications Registry.

425. Government of India Notification (F. No. 12(31)99-IPC (Vol.V)), https://upload.indiacode.nic.in/showfile?actid=AC_CEN_45_75_00001_200037_1517807324048&type=notification&filename=SO%20746.pdf.

426. Government of India Notification (F. No. 15/7/2016-IPR-II), https://copyright.gov.in/Documents/NOTIFICATION%20AND%20ORDER%20REPORTING%20TO%20TRANSFER%20OF%20WORK%20RELATING%20TO%20COPYRIGHT%20.pdf.

Chapter 2. Subject Matter of Protection

408. The Act defines 'semiconductor integrated circuit' to mean a product having transistors or other circuitry elements which are inseparably formed on a semiconductor material or an insulating material and designed to perform an electronic circuitry function.[427]

Under section 2(h), 'layout-design' means a layout of transistors, and other circuitry elements and includes lead wires connecting such elements and expressed in any manner in a semiconductor integrated circuit.

427. Section 2(r).

Chapter 3. Conditions of Protection

409. When an application for the registration of layout-design has been accepted and has not been opposed, and the time for opposition has expired, except where the registration is prohibited under the law, the registration shall be granted from the date of making the said application. Or where the application has been opposed and decided in applicant's favour, except where the registration is prohibited under the law, it shall be granted from the date of making the said application. After registration, the Registrar will issue a certificate of registration in the prescribed form. In case the registration is not completed within twelve months by reason of default on the applicant's part, the application shall stand abandoned after giving notice to the applicant.[428]

410. Section 7 prohibits registration of certain layout-designs, i.e., a design which is not original, or has been commercially exploited, either in India or a convention country, or not inherently distinctive, or not inherently capable of being distinguishable from any other registered layout-design.

428. Section 13.

Chapter 4. Formalities: Procedure for the Grant and Obtaining Protection

411. Section 8 prescribes the procedure for application of registration, wherein any creator of a layout-design shall apply to the Registrar in writing in the prescribed manner for the registration of his/her layout-design. The application has to be filed in the office of the Semiconductor Integrated Circuits Layout-Design Registry within whose territorial limits the principal place of business in India is situated. In case of joint application, the application to be filed in the Registry within whose territorial limits, the principal place of business in India of the first applicant, is situated.

412. After an application for registration of a layout-design has been accepted, the Registrar shall, within fourteen days, accept application to be advertised in the prescribed manner. Where after advertisement of an application, an error in the application has been corrected, or the application has been permitted to be amended, the Registrar may cause the application to be advertised again.[429]

413. Section 11 prescribes the procedure for opposition to registration. Any person can give notice of opposition in writing in the prescribed manner to the Registrar within three months from the date of advertisement/re-advertisement of an application for registration. The Registrar shall serve a copy of the notice on the applicant for registration, who shall send a counterstatement of the grounds for his application, within two months from the receipt of such notice. Failure to do so would result in abandonment of the application. The counterstatement shall be served on the person giving notice of opposition. Both opponent and applicant are to submit evidence in the prescribed manner, and after hearing both, the Registrar shall decide the matter.

429. Section 10.

Chapter 5. Ownership and Transfer

414. The registered proprietor of a layout-design may transfer ownership in such design by way of assignment, licence, mortgage, or the ownership may be transferred by operation of law in the case of transmission, as is provided for in section 21. All such transfers in ownership are required to be registered with the Registrar, under an application in the prescribed form.

Chapter 6. Scope of Exclusive Rights

415. The rights conferred by the Semiconductor Act upon the registered proprietor are the right to obtain relief in respect of any infringement of the registered layout-design and the exclusive right to the use of the layout-design. These rights are independent of the fact as to whether the layout-design is incorporated in an article or not.[430]

In addition, section 19 also states that in all legal proceedings relating to a registered layout-design, the certificate of registration granted under the Act, and all subsequent assignments and transmissions, shall be prima facie evidence of the validity of the layout-design.

430. Section 17.

Chapter 7. Duration of Certificate

416. According to section 15, the registration of a layout-design shall be for a period of ten years from the date of filing an application for registration or from the date of first commercial exploitation anywhere in any country, whichever is earlier.

Chapter 8. Infringement and Remedies

417. A detailed description of the acts that constitute infringement under the Act of 2000 is given in section 18. Section 18 states that a registered layout-design is infringed by a person who, not being the registered proprietor or a registered user thereof:

(a) does any act of reproducing a registered layout-design in its entirety or any part thereof, except reproducing any part which is not original under section 7(2);
(b) does any act of importing or selling or otherwise distributing for commercial purposes a registered layout-design or a semiconductor integrated circuit incorporating such registered layout-design for the use of which such person is not entitled under this Act:
    (1) Section 18 further lists out the exemptions from infringement penalty, i.e. where the acts were done for the purpose of scientific evaluation, analysis, research or teaching.

The penalties prescribed by the Act of 2000, depending on the extent of infringement, include:

(1) injunction;
(2) damages or account of profits;
(3) delivery up of infringing material;
(4) imprisonment of up to three years or a fine from INR 50,000 to INR 1,000,000.

Chapter 9. Prohibitions and Invalidity of Registration of Certain Layout-Designs

418. Section 7 is necessarily to be read with section 62 of the Semiconductor Integrated Circuits Layout-Design Act, 2000, which can be used as a substantial defence. Along with the same, section 61 and section 69 can be used as defences under the act as well.

419. Certain designs are prohibited by the said Act. If the said layout-design:

- is not original;
- which has been commercially exploited anywhere in India or in a convention country;
- which is not inherently distinctive;
- which is not inherently capable of being distinguishable from any other registered layout-design, shall not be registered as a layout-design. Provided that a layout-design which has been commercially exploited for not more than two years from the date on which an application for its registration has been filed either in India or in a convention country shall be treated as not having been commercially exploited;
- where an original layout-design has been created in a contract of employment, the right of registration to such layout-design under the said Act shall belong, in the absence of any contractual provision to the contrary, to the person who commissioned the work or to the employer or the same has already been commercially exploited anywhere in India.

420. No suit or other legal proceedings shall lie against any person in respect of anything which is in good faith done or intended to be done in pursuance of this Act.

Selected Bibliography

Ahuja, V.K. 'Intellectual Property Rights in India', Second Edition, LexisNexis, 2016.
Mittal, D.P. 'Indian Patents Law'. Taxmann, 1999.
Narayanan, P. 'Intellectual Property Law'. Eastern Law House, 1997.
Narayanan, P. 'Copyright and Industrial Designs'. Eastern Law House, 1995.
Shavaksha, K.S. 'The Trade and Merchandise Marks Act, 1958'. Edited by R.K. Abichandani. India: Butterworths, 1999.
Vikas Vashishth. 'Law and Practice of Intellectual Property in India'. Bharat Law House, 1999.
Acts cited in order of appearance
The Copyright Act, 1957 as amended by Copyright (Amendment) Act, 2012.
The Patents Act, 1970 as amended by the Patents Amendment Act, 2005.
The Trademarks Act, 1999.
The Geographical Indications of Goods (Registration & Protection) Act, 1999.
The Designs Act, 2000.
The Protection of Plant Varieties and Farmers' Rights Act, 2001.
The Biological Diversity Act, 2002.
The Semiconductor Integrated Circuit Layout-Design Act, 2000.

Selected Bibliography

Index

The numbers here refer to paragraph numbers.

Index

Index

www.ingramcontent.com/pod-product-compliance
Lightning Source LLC
LaVergne TN
LVHW021930101126
852251LV00023B/260
* 9 7 8 9 4 0 3 5 4 6 3 8 4 *